Python for Beginners

The Crash Course to Learn Programming Python Faster and Remember it Longer. Includes Hands-On Projects and Exercises for Machine Learning, Data Science Analysis, and Artificial Intelligence

Table of Contents

Introduction

Chapter 1: The Benefits of Working with the Python Language

Chapter 2: Installing and Working with Python on Different Operating Systems

Chapter 3: Some of the Basic Parts of the Python Code

Chapter 4: How to Work Classes and Objects

Chapter 5: Creating your Own Inheritance

Chapter 6: Creating a Loop in Python

Chapter 7: Working with the Conditional Statements

Chapter 8: Exception Handling in the Python Language

Chapter 9: Data Analysis with Python

Chapter 10: Can I Test my Code?

Chapter 11: Python and Artificial Intelligence

Chapter 12: Python and Machine Learning

Chapter 13: Practical Codes and Exercises to Use Python

Conclusion

Introduction

Congratulations on downloading Python *for Beginners* and thank you for doing so.

The following chapters will discuss everything that you need to know when it comes to Python coding, and how to use this with data analysis and even machine learning as well. Whether you have worked with other coding languages for a bit, or this is the very first time that you have entered the world of coding, this guidebook has all of the information that you need to get things started with the Python language.

To start this guidebook, we are going to take some time to learn more about the Python language. We will take a look at some of the benefits of the Python code and how you would be able to use this coding language rather than some of the others, how to install Python on the various operating systems that are there, and some of the basic parts of the Python code to help you to get started before we dive into the different parts of this code.

Then we will spend some time to talk about the different options that you can use in order to learn how to do some of your own codings, even as a beginner with Python. Some of the different types of coding that you are able to do with Python and that we are going to discuss in this guidebook includes how to handle classes and objects, how to create some of your own inheritances, how to create a loop in Python, and working with conditional statements and exception handling.

Once we have some of the basics down and we are able to work with some of these basic coding options that come with Python, it is time to move on to some of the machine learning and data analysis that you are able to do with Python. This part of the guidebook is going to focus on how to create your own data analysis, how to test out the codes that you write, how to handle Python and artificial intelligence, and how machine learning and Python can work together. Then we will end this guidebook with some of the practical codes and exercises that you can do with Python in order to create your own machine learning algorithms as well.

There are a lot of benefits of using Python, especially if you want to be able to get into machine learning, artificial intelligence, and data analysis. All of these can be used with other coding languages if you choose, but Python is the easiest and most efficient to get this done. As a beginner, it may seem like it is impossible to learn how to use these and get ahead, but in this guidebook, we are going to spend time looking at how to do all of this and put it all together to get the results that we want. When you are ready to learn some of the basics that come with Python and how to use it with other options like artificial intelligence and machine learning, make sure to check out this guidebook to learn how to get started.

There are plenty of books on this subject on the market, thanks again for choosing this one! Every effort was made to ensure it is full of as much useful information as possible, please enjoy!

Chapter 1: The Benefits of Working with the Python Language

When it comes to picking out the coding language that you want to work with, there are a lot of different options that you can go with. Some are going to provide you with a lot of power. Some are going to work specifically with certain operating systems. And others are going to work the best when it comes to working on a website or online. But one of the best coding languages for you to work with that will help improve your coding experience and will help you to do a lot of different programming applications, then you have to learn how to work with Python.

Python is going to be a great coding language that helps you to really do a good job with many applications online and for programs that you want to make. It is easy enough for a beginner to use, in fact, it was designed to be used by those who are beginners and who have never coded before, while still having the strength that you need to handle some of the different harder applications, such as machine learning, that you would like to explore.

There are a lot of different benefits that come with using the Python language and this is why so many people like to spend time learning how to work with this kind of language. There are some benefits that you are going to enjoy when you decide to learn how to code with Python.

There are a lot of different support libraries that you are able to use. You will be able to find an extension and a library that works with Python for almost anything that you need. These libraries are great for providing you with the algorithms, the functions, and more that you need in order to get any coding task that you want to be done. You can work with just the traditional library that comes with Python originally, or you can go through and work with some of the other extensions and libraries based on the kind of project you would like to do.

Another benefit that comes with this coding language is all of the different integration features that happen. Python can be a good thing to a programmer because it is going to integrate what is known as the Enterprise Application Integration. This is going to be useful because it can make sure that you can work with different operating systems, different coding languages, and more. There is almost nothing that Python isn't able to help you out with, so learning how to use it can be so great.

Python is also going to provide you with more productivity in the process. The language here is going to be designed as an object-oriented language, and it includes many different kinds of support libraries to help you get things done. Because of these resources, and the ease of use that comes with this language, the programmer is going to be able to get more done in a shorter amount of time. This can even help to improve how much productivity the programmer is going to enjoy while using some different coding languages along with Python.

Many programmers like to go with Python because of the amount of ease of use that comes with it. Python was developed so that it could be as easy to use as possible, and the amount of adaptability that comes with it. This is going to mean that the language is easy to learn and makes things easier for even a beginner to work with. This guidebook is going to spend some time on the basics, along with some of the things that may seem a bit more complicated, to make sure that you can create some of the projects that you want in this library.

In addition to this language being easy for a beginner to learn, it is also an easy-to-read kind of language. As you go through the different codes that are found with this guidebook, you will be able to read through it, even before you have really learned it too much. There are not a lot of extras that come with it, and you will be able to read through it in no time at all and it won't take long until you can write some of your own codes as well.

Even though it is easier for a lot of beginners to get started with, it is also going to contain a ton of power behind it. Many of those who decide to work with Python is going to be impressed by all of the power that is in this kind of coding language thanks to how easy it is. Even as a beginner language, it is going to contain all of the power that you need to combine with many other languages, and to do almost any kind of application that you want.

The community that comes with this language is also something special that you will love. Python is one of the top languages for programming and coding that are available, which is good news for those who are just getting started. All of the people who are able to use this program can answer your questions, show you different kinds of codes that you can write, and so much more.

And finally, you will enjoy that the Python code is going to be open-sourced. What this means is that you are able to get the basics of Python and a lot of the libraries and extensions that you need with this language for free. There are developers who are working on this language on a constant basis, but you will still be able to use it and download it on your computer for free.

As you can see, there are a lot of benefits that come with working with the Python language, rather than one of the other coding languages that are available. And this is a big reason why so many programmers choose to go with this kind of language over one of the others. Whether it is the first time that you have ever decided to code, or you have been coding for some time, you will find that the Python language is going to be one of the best for you to choose.

Chapter 2: Installing and Working with Python on Different Operating Systems

Now that you have decided to work with the Python code to help you to do some of your own programming and coding, it is time to get to work with installing this on your computer. You will not be able to get all of the work done or use any of the coding languages if all of the different parts and files that come with the Python code are on your computer. This chapter is going to take some time to look at how you can install Python on your computer, no matter which operating system you want to work with.

For these steps, we are going to assume that you are getting Python from www.python.org. There are other resources where you are able to get this programming language, but this one is often the easiest because it is going to have all of the files and extensions that you need to make Python work, and all of them are free to use. Other sources can provide some more features and other things that you need, but they do not always work well, or they may be missing some of the parts that you need. So, let's dive in and see how we can get the folders of Python set up with our computer.

Installing on the Mac OS X

The first option that we are going to look at when we want to add on Python to our operating system is the Mac OS X. This is a popular option when it comes to the operating system on a computer, and it is going to work just fine with some of the codings that we decide to do with Python. However, you need to double-check the system because some of Python versions are going to automatically be included on this operating system. To see which version of the Python program is found on your system, it will include the following code:

Python – V

This is going to show you the version you get so a number will come up. You can also choose to install Python 3 on this system if you would like, and it isn't required to uninstall the 2.X version on the computer. To check for the 3.X installation, you just need to open up the terminal app and then type in the following prompt:

Python3 – V

The default on OS X is that Python 3 is not going to be installed at all. If you want to use Python 3, you can install it using some of the installers that are on Python.org. This is a good place to go from because it will install everything that you need to write and execute your codes with Python. It will have the Python shell, the IDLE development tools, and the interpreter. Unlike what happens with Python 2.X, these tools are installed as a standard application in the Applications folder.

Being able to run the IDLE and the Python shell is going to be dependent on which version you choose and some of your own personal preferences. You can use the following commands to help you start the shell and IDLE applications:

- For Python 2.X just type in "Idle"
- For Python 3.X, just type in "Idle3"

Installing on a Windows System

A Windows system is also able to work with Python. There is not going to be a version of this program on Windows though simply because the Windows system has its own programming language that you are able to work with. This does not mean that you are limited to only using that language, but it does mean that you are going to have to spend some time installing Python and picking out the version of Python that you would like to use.

There are a few steps that you are able to use in order to make sure that you can install the Python program on your system. It can look a bit intimidating when you first get started, but you will find that these steps only take a few minutes, so it isn't as bad as it seems. Some of the steps that you need to follow in order to make sure that Python is installed properly on your Windows computer will include:

1. To get started with this, it is time to visit the official download page for Python and then grab the Windows Installer. You are able to choose which version of Python that you would like to work with. Your default of this is going to give you the 32-bit version of the language, but you can go through and click on the 64-bit version if this is what you need for your computer system.
2. Now you can go through and push on the right-click button on the installer and then allow it to Run as Administrator. There are going to be a point that gives you two options. You will want to go with the button that allows for customizing the installation.
3. On the following screen, you need to make sure that you look under the part for Optional Features and click on all of the

boxes that are there. When those boxes are filled out, you can click the Next button.

4. While you are still in the part for Advanced Options, you can pick out the location where you would like to install Python. Click on Install and then wait a few minutes in order to get this installation finished. Then close out of the installer when it is all done.

5. At this point, you can set up the PATH variable to the system to make sure that it is going to include all of the directories that come with the packages and to make sure that all of the other components that you need show up as well. The steps that you can follow to make all of this happen includes:

    a. Start this part by opening up your Control Panel. This is easily done by clicking on your taskbar and then typing in "Control Panel". Click on the icon that shows up.

    b. While you are inside this part of the process, it is time to do a search for the Environment. Then you can click on the part that allows you to edit the System Environment Variables. From here, you can then click on the button that allows you to enter into Environment Variables.

c. Head over to the section that is for User Variables. You can choose to edit the PATH variable that is already there for your use, or you can decide to create a brand new one.

d. If you see that this system doesn't provide you with a variable for the PATH, then it is time to create your own. You can create this by clicking on NEW. Make the name of the PATH variable and add in the directories that you want. Close all the control Panel dialogs and then click on Next to finish it up.

6. At this point, you are able to open up the command prompt on your Windows computer. This is done by clicking on your Start Menu and then going to the Windows

System and then into Command Prompt. Type in the word "python". This will make sure that the interpreter of Python is going to load up for you.

At this point, the program is going to be set up and ready to use on your Windows system. You can choose to open up the other parts of the system as well to make sure that all of the parts that you need are in one place, and then it is time to write out any code that you want when the time is right.

How to install Python on your Linux System

Now that we have been able to explore how to install Python on your Windows computer and your Mac OS X, it is time to move on to some of the steps that you can use to get this language installed on your Linux system as well. There are many individuals and programmers alike who are moving over to the Linux system, so it is one that we need to spend some time learning how to use for our needs.

The first thing to do here is to see if there is a version of Python 3 already on your system. You can open up the command prompt on Linux and then run the following code:

```
$ python3 - - version
```

If you are on Ubuntu 16.10 or newer, then it is a simple process to install Python 3.6. You just need to use the following commands:

```
$ sudo apt-get update
$ sudo apt-get install Python3.6
```

If you are relying on an older version of Ubuntu or another version, then you may want to work with the deadsnakes PPA, or another tool, to help you download the Python 3.6 version. The code that you need to do this includes:

```
$ sudo apt-get install software-properties-common
$ sudo add-apt repository ppa:deadsnakes/ppa
# suoda apt-get update
```

$ sudo apt-get install python3.6

The thing to remember here is that if you have spent some time working with a few of the other distributions that come with Linux, it is likely that your system is going to have a version of Python 3 already installed on there. If you do not see this here, you can choose to use the package manager of the distribution. Or you can go through the steps that we have above in order to help you to install any version of Python that you want before using the program.

Understanding the Interpreter in Python

The standard installation of Python, when you do it on python.org, is going to contain documentation, information on licensing, and three main files to execute that help you develop and then run the scripts that you run on python. These include the Python interpreter, IDLE, and Shell.

First is the Python interpreter. This is important because it is responsible for executing the scripts that you decide to write. The interpreter can convert the .py script files into instructions and then processes them according to the type of code that you write in the file.

Then there is the Python IDLE. This is known as the integrated development and learning environment. It is going to contain all of the tools that are needed to develop your programs in Python. You will find tools for debugging, the text editor, and the shell with this. Depending on the version of Python that you choose, the IDLE can either be extensive or pretty basic. You can also pick out your own IDLE if there is another version that you like better. Many people like to find new text editors because they think the one with Python doesn't have the right features, but the one from Python is just fine for the codes we will do so it's not necessary to pick a different one.

Then there is the Python Shell. This is an interactive command line-driven interface that is found in the interpreter. This is going to hold onto the commands that you decide to write out. If the shell understands what you are writing, then it will go through and execute the code that you write. But if it doesn't understand the code, or you write it out incorrectly, then it will return an error message to you.

All of these can be important when it comes to writing out your code. When working with the installation through python.org, they will be installed for you and you won't need to go through and do any other work to make it happen. If you get the Python version from some other location, check the files that you get and see if you need to make some changes or add these onto your computer to write your code.

Chapter 3: Some of the Basic Parts of the Python Code

Now that we have learned a bit more about the Python code, and some of the things that you need to do in order to get this coding language set up on your computer, it is time to take a look at some of the different things that you can do with your code. We are going to start out with some of the basics, and then will build on this when we get a bit further on in this guidebook to see some of the other things that we are able to do with this language. With this in mind, let's take a look at some of the basics that you need to know about any code in Python, and all that you are going to be able to do with this coding language.

The Keywords in Python

The first part of the Python code that we are going to focus on is the Python keywords. These keywords are going to be reserved because they give the commands over to the compiler. You do not want to let these keywords show up in other parts of the code, and it is important to know that you are using them in the right part of the code.

Any time that you are using these keywords in the wrong manner, or in the wrong part of the code, you are going to end up with some errors in place. These keywords are going to be there to tell your compiler what you wanted to happen, allowing it to know what it should do at the different parts of the code. They are really important to the code and will make sure that everything works the proper manner and at the right times.

How To Name The Identifiers in your Code?

The next thing that we need to focus on for a moment when it comes to your code is working with the identifiers. There are a lot of different identifiers that you are able to work with, and they do come in a variety of names including classes, variables, entities, and functions. The neat thing that happens when you go through the process of naming an identifier is that the same rules are going to apply no matter what name you have, which can make it easier for a beginner to remember the different rules that come with them.

So, let's dive into some of the rules that we need to remember when doing these identifiers. You have a lot of different options to keep in mind when you decide to name the identifiers. For example, you can rely on using all kinds of letters, whether they are lowercase or uppercase. Numbers work well, too. You will be allowed to bring in the underscore symbol any time that you would like. And any combination of these together can help you to finish up the naming that you want to do.

One thing to remember with the naming rules though is that you should not start the name with any kind of number, and you do not want to allow any kind of space between the words that you are writing out. So, you would not want to pick out the name of 5kids, but you could call it fivekids. And five kids for a name would not work, but five_kids would be fine.

When you are working on the name for any of the identifiers that you want to create in this kind of coding language, you need to make sure that you are following the rules above, but add to this that the name you choose has to be one that you are able to remember later. You are going to need to, at some point, pull that name back up, and if you picked out one that is difficult to remember or doesn't make sense in the code that you are doing, and you can't call it back up, it is going to raise an error or another problem along the way. Outside of these rules, you will be fine naming the identifier anything that makes sense for that part of the code.

How to Handle the Control Flow with Python

The control flow in this language can be important. This control flow is there to ensure that you wrote out the code the proper way. There are some types of strings in your code that you may want to write out so that the compiler can read them the right way. But if you write out the string in the wrong manner, you are going to end up with errors in the system. We will take a look at many codes into this guidebook that follows the right control flow for this language, which can make it easier to know what you need to get done and how you can write out codes in this language.

The Python Statements

The next topic that we need to take a look at when we do some of our codings is the idea of the statements. These are going to be a simple thing to work on when it comes to Python. They are simply going to be strings of code that you are able to write out, and then you will tell the compiler to show that string on the computer string at the right time.

When you give the compiler the instructions that it needs to follow, you will find that there are going to be statements that come with it. As long as you write these statements out in the right manner, the compiler is going to be able to read them and will show the message that you have chosen on the computer screen. You are able to choose to write these statements out as long or as short as you would like, and it all is going to depend on the kind of code that you are trying to work on at the time.

The Importance of the Python Comments

Any time that you are writing out new code in Python, it is important to know how to work with the comments. You may find that as you are working on the various parts of your code, and changing things around, you may want to add a note or name a part of the code or leave any other explanation that helps to know what that part of the code is all about. These notes are things that you and anyone else who is reading through the code will be able to see and utilize, but they are not going to affect the code. The compiler knows that comment is going on and will just skip that and go to the next part of the code that you wrote out.

Making your own comment in Python is a pretty easy process. You just need to add in the # symbol before the note that you want to write, and then the compiler knows that a note is there and that it doesn't need to read that part of the code at all. It is possible for you to go through and add in as many of these comments to the code that you are writing as you would like and you could fill up the whole code with comments. The compiler would be able to handle this, but the best coding practice is to just add in the amount that you really need. This helps to keep things organized and ensures that you are going to have things looking nice and neat.

Variables in Python

Variables are another part of the code that you will need to know about because they are so common in your code. The variables are there to help store some of the values that you place in the code, helping them to stay organized and nice. You can easily add in some of the values to the right variable simply by using the equal sign. It is even possible for you to take two values and add them to the same variables if you want and you will see this occur in a few of the codes that we discuss through this guidebook. Variables are very common, and you will easily see them throughout the examples that we show.

Looking for the Operators

Another part of the code that we can focus on when working in the Python language is the idea of the operators. These are simple to use, and there are going to be a lot of the codes that you try to work on that will include these operators. But even though they are pretty easy to work with, they can add to a level of power that is so important to a lot of the codes that you want. And there are a variety of operators that you are able to focus on when you write a Python code, so you have some options.

For example, you can start out with the arithmetic functions. These are good ones to work with any time that you need to do some kind of mathematics with your code. There are going to be the assignment operators that make sure a value is assigned over to the variable that you are working on. There can be comparison operators as well which allow you to take two parts of the code, or the code and the input from the user, and then compare them to see if they are the same or not and then reacting in the way that you would like based on the code that you wrote.

As you can see, there are a ton of different parts that come with the basics of the Python code. Many of these are going to be seen in the types of codes that you are trying to write out in Python and can really help you to start writing out some of your own codes. As we go through some of the examples, as well as the practice exercises, as we go through this guidebook, you will find that these basics are going to be found in a lot of the codes that you would like to work on.

Chapter 4: How to Work Classes and Objects

One of the things that you will really enjoy working on when it comes to Python is the organization that comes with it. This kind of coding language is going to spend time dividing everything up into classes and objects. This allows for more organization, ensures that every part of the code has a place and won't get lost, and really makes it easier for the beginner programmer to get things done without as much hassle.

Before we go through and create a new class, it is time to look a bit closer at what these classes and objects are all about. The objects are going to be anything that you are able to find in the real world. You will have a lot of objects that can work in the Python language, and these are going to help to power the code that you are working with, and will ensure that your code behaves in the manner that you would like. You can have any kind of object that you want, and they would match one of the objects that you want to do in the real world.

And then we have the classes. The best way to think about the classes in our Python code is as a little box that holds onto those objects that you created before. This helps to provide us with some organization when it comes to the code because we can place all of the objects that we want into each class, and then easily pull them back out at a later time when we want.

You can make as many classes as you would like in the code, and you get the benefit of being able to add in any objects, and as many objects, as you would like into each class. The biggest thing to remember here is that you need to make sure that the objects that belong to each class go together and make sense together. If someone else came in and looked at the coding that you did, and looked into one of the classes, would they be able to tell why all of those objects were found in the same class?

This doesn't mean that all of the objects in one class has to be exactly the same. But they need to make sense out of it as much as possible. You do not have to have a class that is just cars, for example, unless you would like to have it this way. But you could also go with a class that is going to contain different vehicles and this would be just fine as well.

How to Create a Class

With the information behind us about what these classes and objects are all about, it is time for us to take a look at the steps that we need to follow in order to create one of our own classes along the way. It is important to learn how to create our own classes because it is going to make sure that we have everything in place, and we won't lose anything at the same time.

To make sure that you get the class ready to go, you need to put the right kind of keyword in place and then go through and name the class. You get the freedom here to give the class any name that you would like, but it is important to come up with a name that makes sense, and you have to place the name after the keyword so that the compiler knows what is going on.

After naming the class, it is time to name a subclass, which will be placed inside parenthesis to stick with proper programming rules. Make sure that at the end of that first line, whenever you create a class, that you add in a semicolon. While this isn't technically needed with most newer versions of Python and the code is going to work even if you forget this part, it is still considered part of coding etiquette to do this so make sure that you put it in.

Writing a class sounds more complicated than it really is, so let's stop here and look at an example of how you would write this out in Python. Then we can discuss what the parts mean and why they are important. A good example of creating a class with Python includes the following:

class Vehicle(object):

```python
#constructor
def _init_(self, steering, wheels, clutch, breaks, gears):
    self._steering = steering
    self._wheels = wheels
    self._clutch = clutch
    self._breaks = breaks
    self._gears = gears
#destructor
def _del_(self):
    print("This is destructor....")

#member functions or methods
def Display_Vehicle(self):
    print('Steering:' , self._steering)
    print('Wheels:', self._wheels)
    print('Clutch:', self._clutch)
    print('Breaks:', self._breaks)
    print('Gears:', self._gears)
#instantiate a vehicle option
myGenericVehicle = Vehicle('Power Steering', 4, 'Super Clutch', 'Disk Breaks', 5)

myGenericVehicle.Display_Vehicle()
```

To see how this is going to work well for your needs and how the class can be set up, you should open up your compiler and type in the code that we have above. This will ensure that you are going to be able to test out the code and see which kind of class you have been able to create. This is a simple code that ensures we have the right objects that go into the different class that we assigned, and will make sure that when we open up that class, it is all going to open up and work the way that we would like.

How to access some of the members of our class

As you look at the code that we wrote above, you can see that we took some time to go through and create a class and then added in a few objects to this as well. This is going to make it so that our objects are in the same place and can make it easier to pull them all out and make them easier to use in the long run. But now that the class is done, it is time to look at some of the objects that we put into that class and then learn how to pull them out.

In this part of the code, we have to learn the steps that are needed to access members of that class that we were able to create above. You want to make sure that your text editor and your compiler will be able to recognize all of the classes that you design later on because this is going to ensure that both of those are able to execute the code in the right manner.

Now, to set up the code that you want to right, you need to make sure that you set it up right, and there are a few methods that work for this. We are going to look at the accessor method to get this done because it is the easiest in most cases, and it is the one that most programmers are going to work with as well. To understand how you would use the method of the accessor function, look at the code below to help you get started:

class Cat(object)
    itsAge = None

itsWeight = None

itsName = None

#set accessor function use to assign values to the fields or member vars

def setItsAge(self, itsAge):

self.itsAge = itsAge

def setItsWeight(self, itsWeight):

self.itsWeight = itsWeight

def setItsName(self, itsName):

self.itsName =itsName

#get accessor function use to return the values from a field

def getItsAge(self):

return self.itsAge

def getItsWeight(self):

return self.itsWeight

def getItsName(self):

return self.itsName

objFrisky = Cat()

objFrisky.setItsAge(5)
objFrisky.setItsWeight(10)
objFrisky.setItsName("Frisky")
print("Cats Name is:", objFrisky.getItsname())
print("Its age is:", objFrisky.getItsAge())
print("Its weight is:", objFrisky.getItsName())

Classes are not meant to be difficult to work with. They are perfect for helping you to take care of your information and keep it in order so that it makes the most sense. You can create any kind of class that you would like and fill it up with any objects that you like, as long as those objects match each other in some way. Both the objects and classes are going to make a difference in your code to keep it organized, easy to read, and working properly.

Chapter 5: Creating your Own Inheritance

The next topic of coding in Python that we are going to take a look at is known as the inheritance. This is going to seem a bit complicated in the beginning, but it is a great way for you to work on developing some of your coding skills, and will make it easier for you to reuse parts of your code and save some of the coding and the mess that can come from rewriting out all of the different parts that you usually would.

Working with these inheritances is a good way to make sure that your code gets the enhancements that you want inside of Python. These inheritances are going to save us time and can make sure that the ending coding that we want is nicer looking and cleaner in the long run. These inheritances are going to help you to take some of the code that you wrote out earlier and reuse them without having to spend so much time rewriting them out over and over again. Remember that these are going to be unique to Python and other OOP languages, and can be one of the perks of this kind of language.

To keep things as simple as possible, when you are working with the inheritance, you are going to work with the parent code, which is the original code that you want to copy, and then move it down into the new part of the code, making changes to the parts that you want, and then reusing the parts that you like. You can use this to help move the code forward without rewriting it, or just to make the code stronger in some cases. Even as a beginner, it is possible to use these inheritances to help you reuse the code as much as you need to, without having to waste time and room rewriting it out each time.

During the process of working with an inheritance, you would make sure that you take the parent code and then get it all copied over to some other part of the program that you need. The new part that you create is going to be the child code, and it is unique because you can pick and choose which parts of the parent code you would like to keep and which parts you are going to throw out. you can go through this process as many times as you would like to get the code to behave properly.

To help make more sense out of these inheritances, how they work, and how they can help to keep your code clean and tidy and save you time, let's take a look at an example of how they look in your code:

```
#Example of inheritance
#base class
class Student(object):
    def __init__(self, name, rollno):
        self.name = name
        self.rollno = rollno
#Graduate class inherits or derived from Student class
class GraduateStudent(Student):
    def __init__(self, name, rollno, graduate):
        Student __init__(self, name, rollno)
        self.graduate = graduate

def DisplayGraduateStudent(self):
```

```python
print"Student Name:", self.name)
print("Student Rollno:", self.rollno)
print("Study Group:", self.graduate)

#Post Graduate class inherits from Student class
class PostGraduate(Student):
    def __init__(self, name, rollno, postgrad):
        Student__init__(self, name, rollno)
        self.postgrad = postgrad

    def DisplayPostGraduateStudent(self):
        print("Student Name:", self.name)
        print("Student Rollno:", self.rollno)
        print("Study Group:", self.postgrad)

#instantiate from Graduate and PostGraduate classes
objGradStudent = GraduateStudent("Mainu", 1, "MS-Mathematics")
objPostGradStudent = PostGraduate("Shainu", 2, "MS-CS")
objPostGradStudent.DisplayPostGraduateStudent()
```

When you type this into your interpreter, you are going to get the results:

('Student Name:', 'Mainu')
('Student Rollno:', 1)
('Student Group:', 'MSC-Mathematics')
('Student Name:', 'Shainu')
('Student Rollno:', 2)
('Student Group:', 'MSC-CS')

You are able to go through this process and use the base or parent class as many times as you would like. It is easy to go down the line as many times as your code asks for, making changes along the way without worrying about ruining up any of the parent code along the way. As long as you do not work on a circular inheritance here, you will be fine to keep adding in the base classes down to the child class, and you will be able to get things to change and stay the same as much as you want as well.

Inheritances can be nice because they allow you to keep using a part of the code that you already created in order to create new parts of your code. This can keep the program code looking nice and saves you a lot of time in the process. Learning how to work with these inheritances will help you to really enhance your codes, keeps it all set up and clean, and will ensure that your codes will work the way that you want.

Chapter 6: Creating a Loop in Python

Loops are going to be next on the list of topics we need to explore when we are working with Python. These are going to be a great way to clean up some of the code that you are working on so that you can add in a ton of information and processing in the code, without having to go through the process of writing out all those lines of code. For example, if you would like a program that would count out all of the numbers that go from one to one hundred, you would not want to write out that many lines of code along the way. Or if you would like to create a program for doing a multiplication table, this would take forever as well. But doing a loop can help to get all of this done in just a few lines of code, saving you a lot of time and code writing in the process.

It is possible to add in a lot of different information into the loops that you would like to write, but even with all of this information, they are still going to be easy to work with. These loops are going to have all of the ability to tell your compiler that it needs to read through the same line of code, over and over again, until the program has reached the conditions that you set. This helps to simplify the code that you are working on while still ensuring that it works the way that you want when executing it.

As you decide to write out some of these loops, it is important to remember to set up the kind of condition that you would like to have met before you ever try to run the program. If you just write out one of these loops, without this condition, the loop won't have any idea when it is time to stop and will keep going on and on. Without this kind of condition, the code is going to keep reading through the loop and will freeze your computer. So, before you execute this code, double-check that you have been able to put in these conditions before you try to run it at all.

As you go through and work on these loops and you are creating your own Python code, there are going to be a few options that you can use with loops. There are a lot of options but we are going to spend our time looking at the three main loops that most programmers are going to use, the ones that are the easiest and most efficient.

The while loop

Out of the three loops that we are going to discuss in this guidebook, we are going to start out with the while loop. The while loop is going to be one that will tell the compiler the specific times that you would like it to go through with that loop. This could be a good loop to use any time that you want the compiler to count from one to ten. With this example, your condition would tell the compiler to stop when it reaches ten, so that it doesn't freeze and keep going. This is also a good option that programmers like to work with because it will make sure that it goes through the code at least one time, if not more before it decides to head on to the other parts of the code that you are writing. To see a good example of how you can work with the while loop take a look at the code that we have below for reference:

```
#calculation of simple interest. Ask the user to input the principal, rate of interest, number of years.

counter = 1
while(counter <= 3):
    principal = int(input("Enter the principal amount:"))
    numberofyeras = int(input("Enter the number of years:"))
    rateofinterest = float(input("Enter the rate of interest:"))
    simpleinterest = principal * numberofyears * rateofinterest/100
    print("Simple interest = %.2f" %simpleinterest)
    #increase the counter by 1
    counter = counter + 1
    print("You have calculated simple interest for 3 time!")
```

This example allows your user to go through and place the information that pertains to them inside the program. The code will them computer the interest rates based on the information that the user provides. For this one, we set up the while (right at the beginning of the code) and told it to only go through the loop three times. You can change it to go through the process as many times as you would like.

The for loop

Now that we have had some time to look at the while loop, it is time to take a look at what is known as the for loop and how we are able to use this in some of the codings that we want to do. When you would like to bring out the for loop there are going to be some differences compared to the while loop from before. Keep in mind here that most programmers are going to consider the for loop the traditional form of coding. You can use this one in many of the situations where you would work with the while loop so it is important to learn how to use this for your needs.

When you are ready to create your own for loop, the user is not going to be the one who would go through here and provide the code with information that is needed to start the loop. Rather than having this happen, the for loop is set up to go through an iteration in whatever order you put it into the code. There is no need to have this kind of input from the user because the loop is set up to just go through the full iteration until it reaches the end. To see how the for loop works, and how it is going to be different from the while loop that we talked about above, take a look at the code below:

 # Measure some strings:
words = ['apple', 'mango', 'banana', 'orange']
for w in words:
print(w, len(w))

Write this code into your compiler and then execute it. The for loop is going to make sure that all the words in the line above it are shown up on the screen, exactly how you wrote them out. If you want them in a different order, you need to do that as you work on the code, not later on. You can add in any words or other information that you want to show up in this kind of loop, just make sure that you have it in the right order from the beginning.

The nested loop

And the third type of loop that we are going to take a look at is known as the nested loop. If you are working on a code that needs a nested loop, you will take either the for loop or the while loop and you will take that one and place it into another loop. In the code, both of these are going to end up running at the same time, and it is going to continue on in this manner until both of these codes are all the way done.

There are a lot of situations where the nested loop is going to be useful and you will want to add it into your code to get things done. A good example of how this is going to work is when you would like to create a multiplication table. The code that can be useful to help you to make your own multiplication table in the Python language with the help of the nested loop would be the following:

 # write a multiplication table from 1 to 10
For x in xrange(1, 11):
    For y in xrange(1, 11):
    Print '%d = %d' % (x, y, x*x)

When you got the output of this program, it is going to look similar to this:

1*1 = 1
1*2 = 2
1*3 = 3
1*4 = 4
All the way up to 1*10 = 2
Then it would move on to do the table by twos such as this:
2*1 =2
2*2 = 4

And so on until you end up with 10*10 = 100 as your final spot in the sequence

Any time you need to get one loop to run inside another loop, the nested loop will be able to help you get this done. You can combine together the for loop, the while loop, or each combination based on what you want to get done inside the code. But it definitely shows you how much time and space inside the code that these loops can save. The multiplication table above only took up four lines to write out and you got a huge table. Think of how long this would take if you had to write out each part of the table!

The for loop, the while loop, and the nested loop are the most common types of loops that beginners will use when writing their own codes in Python. You can use these codes to get a lot of work done in your chosen program without having to write out as many lines. You can use it to make sure that a certain part of your code will go through and rewrite itself.

Chapter 7: Working with the Conditional Statements

There are going to be times when you will work on a program in Python where you will need the program to make some decisions for you, without you being there to tell it how to answer each response that it gets. You can set up the conditions that need to be met to help out with this but there is a lot of unknown when the user is allowed to add in any input that they want, and the conditional statements are going to help you learn how to do this. Since you are not able to handle or guess all of the answers or inputs that the user may give, and so these conditional statements are going to be there to help you get things done.

You will find that these conditional statements are going to be a bit different than what you are used to, but they can work on a lot of different programs that you try to write. They are simple, but it is easy to add to them and change things up so that you

59

are able to get more done, and you can handle any of the answers that your users decide to use

When it comes to working with these conditional statements, there are going to be three options that you are able to work with. These are the if statement, the elif statement, and the if else statement. These are all important, but they are going to work in slightly different ways in order to help you to get some of the codings that you want to be done. Let's explore how each of these is going to work inside your own code.

Starting with the if statement

Out of the conditional statements, the most basic of the three and the one that we are going to focus on first is going to be the if statement. The if statement is a basic conditional statement, and sometimes is going to seem too simple to use on a regular basis. In fact, it is more common that you are going to work with the if else statement or the elif statement when in this kind of field, but it is still important to learn how to work with the if statement so that we get some of the basics that come with this kind of conditional statement:

You can probably already guess that this will cause some problems with most codes, but it is still important to know how to use these statements. A simple code that you can work with for these conditional statements include:

age = int(input("Enter your age:"))
if (age <=18):
    print("You are not eligible for voting, try next election!")
print("Program ends")

There are a few things that will show up with this code. If you have a user go to the program and state that their age is under 18, then the program will work and display the message that is listed there. The user can read this message and then end the program right there.

Now one thing to notice here is that there is a chance for things to not go as planned when you are working with this kind of code. If the user wants to put in an answer for their age that is 18 or higher, then the code is not set up at this point to handle this issue. Right now, the program is going to only list out the message that you have when the user puts their age in as something under 18. But if they wrote out their age as something higher, then it is not going to meet up with the conditions that you have, and nothing will happen.

Of course, we do not want to have a code where only one answer is right, at least now when it comes to the age of the person using the program. They want to be able to put in their real age at the time, and this may or may not be below 18. You want to make sure that your program is working the way that you want, and this is why we will move on to the if else statements.

Moving on to the if else statements

While the if statements are a good place to get some practice when it comes to writing your own codes in Python, there are not going to be a ton of times in programming when you would want to use these at all. It is likely that you don't want to leave the screen empty with nothing there for the user to see. And this is why we want to learn how to work with the if else statement to handle the issues from above.

The if else statement is going to take the things that we have looked at in the if statement, but moves them along another step so they make more sense and can handle more situations. With the example that we had worked on before, the user is going to be able to see the message we had before if they put in any age under 18. But then this goes a bit further because it is also going to provide us with a message if the user is older than 18 as well. This if else statement is going to make sure that the user is going to get some kind of message, no matter what age they put into the system at the time.

With the voting example that we had above, you can implement the following code to make an if else statement:

```
age = int(input("Enter your age:"))
if (age <=18):
        print("You are not eligible for voting, try next election!")
else
        print("Congratulations! You are eligible to vote. Check out your local polling station to find out more information!)
print("Program ends")
```

With this option, you are adding in the else statement, which will cover every age that doesn't fall under 18. This way, if the user does list that as their age, something will still pull up on the screen for them. This can provide you with more freedom when working on your code and you can even add in a few more layers to this. If you want to divide it up so that you get four or five age groups and each one gets a different response, you simply need to add in more if statements to make it happen. The else statement is at the end to catch everything else.

We can take this a bit further to see how things go. Let's say that we want to create a code using the if else statement in order to ask our users what their favorite color is. You would continue on with the if statements based on the colors you would like to choose. You are not able to list out all of the colors that are available because this would take forever and be hard to work on but maybe you choose five colors and give them if statements with a message that is attached.

Then, if the user doesn't pick one of those five colors that you put an if statement with, it will be caught by the else statement as well. This ensures that all answers are caught and responded to, without having to worry about listing out and guessing all of the different possibilities that the user can put in.

Finishing it out with the elif statements

Now that we have had some time to explore a bit with the if statement and the if else statement, it is time to take a look at how the elif statement is going to be the same or different, and how you can use it in your code. You will find that these add in a different kind of level to the codes that you are writing, but they still have ease of use to them.

It is possible to write in as many of the elif statements as you would like to the code, and then you also need to add in the else statement, as we did above with the if else statement, to cover any of the other decisions that need to be handled in the code. You can think of the elif statement like something similar to some of the older games out there, the ones that had a menu of options and allowed the user to pick from one of these. This is pretty similar to how we are going to set up our elif statements.

When you are working on these elif statements, you are able to add in as many different options as you would like to finish it up. Sometimes, you may just add one, two, or three, but you are not limited by this and can add in as many as you would like. Keep in mind though that the more elif statements that you add into the code, the messier it gets and the more that you have to write out. To see how the coding for the elif statements is going to work, make sure to check out the following code:

Print("Let's enjoy a Pizza! Ok, let's go inside Pizzahut!")
print("Waiter, Please select Pizza of your choice from the menu")
pizzachoice = int(input("Please enter your choice of Pizza:"))
if pizzachoice == 1:
    print('I want to enjoy a pizza napoletana')
elif pizzachoice == 2:
    print('I want to enjoy a pizza rustica')
elif pizzachoice == 3:
    print('I want to enjoy a pizza capricciosa')
else:
    print("Sorry, I do not want any of the listed pizza's, please bring a Coca Cola for me.")

With this option, the user is able to choose the type of pizza they want to enjoy, but you can use the same syntax for anything you need in your code. If the user pushes the number 2 in the code, they are going to get a pizza Rustica. If they don't like any of the options, then they are telling the program that they just want to have something to drink, in this case, a Coca Cola.

This is a simple way to use elif statements to give the user a set of choices. In the other options, the user could add in any choice that they wanted, but in the elif statement, they can either pick that they want one of the choices that you provide, or they will have to go with the default option at the end. This can work well for many games that you may want to pick, for some tests online, and other programs where you want to limit the choices that the user gets to pick from in the code.

As you can see, there are a lot of different things that you are able to do when working on these conditional statements. You are able to choose what conditions you would like to have in place, and then make sure that the program is going to behave in the right way the whole time. You can choose whether the if statement, the if else statement or the elif statement is going to be the right one for you, and then add these to the code that you are writing.

Chapter 8: Exception Handling in the Python Language

The next topic that we need to spend some time exploring in this guidebook is the idea of exception handling. There are going to be times when your code tries to show up some errors or other problem inside the code that you are doing, and this is where the exception is going to occur. Knowing when to recognize these exceptions, how to handle them, and even how to make some of your own can make a big difference in how well you are able to do some of your own coding in Python.

These exceptions are going to be brought up by the compiler in a lot of different situations, and sometimes, they are going to look like a simple error message like you may have seen on your own computer before. It is important to really read through any of these exceptions that come up in your code and read through them so that you can learn what they are about, and how you can handle them properly at the same time. This isn't meant to be something to scare you, but there are things that you can do to handle these exceptions and to make sure that you are going to be able to handle them in the proper manner.

Now, there are going to be a few exceptions that are already recognized inside the library that you are using in Python. If you want to write out a code with them in there, or if you find that the user is trying to do something that isn't proper for your program, then the compiler is going to send out an exception about this in order to get it to stop. In some cases, the program you are writing is going to need some extra limitations in place to handle it, and you can raise up, after creating, your own exception.

A good example of an exception that your compiler is automatically going to raise up is when you or the user is to divide it by zero. The compiler is then going to recognize that this is something the user is not able to do, and it is going to send out that exception as an alert. It can also be something that is going to be called up if you, as the programmer, are trying to call up a function and the name is not spelled in the proper manner so there is no match present to bring up.

There are a few different exceptions that are automatically found in your Python library. It is a good idea to take some time to look through them and recognize these exceptions so you can recognize them later on. Some of the most common exceptions that you need to worry about include:

- Finally—this is the action that you will want to use to perform cleanup actions, whether the exceptions occur or not.
- Assert—this condition is going to trigger the exception inside of the code
- Raise—the raise command is going to trigger an exception manually inside of the code.
- Try/except—this is when you want to try out a block of code and then it is recovered

thanks to the exceptions that either you or the Python code raised.

Raising an Exception

The first thing that we need to take a look at, now that we know a bit more about these exceptions and what they mean, is how to write one out, and some of the steps that you can use if one of these does end up in your own code. If you are going through some of the code writing, and you start to notice that an exception will be raised, know that often the solution is going to be a simple one. But as the programmer, you need to take the time to get this fixed. To help us get started here, let's take a look at what the syntax of the code for raising an exception is all about.

x = 10
y = 10
result = x/y #trying to divide by zero
print(result)

The output that you are going to get when you try to get the interpreter to go through this code would be:

>>>
Traceback (most recent call last):
   File "D: \Python34\tt.py", line 3, in <module>
   result = x/y
ZeroDivisionError: division by zero
>>>

As we take a moment to look at the example that we have here, we can see that the program is going to bring up an exception for us, mainly because we are trying to divide a number by zero and this is something that is not allowed in the Python code (and any other coding language for that matter). If you decide not to make any changes at this point, and you go ahead and run the program as it is, you could end up with the compiler sending you an error message. The code is going to tell the user the problem, but as you can see, the problem is not listed out in an easy-to-understand method and it is likely the user will have no idea what is going on or how they can fix the problem at all.

With that example that we worked on above, you have some options. You can choose to leave the message that is kind of confusing if you don't know any coding, or you can add in a new message that is easier to read and explains why this error has been raised in the first place. It won't have a lot of numbers and random letters that only make sense to someone who has done coding for a bit, which makes the whole thing a bit more user-friendly overall. The syntax that you can use to control the message that your user is going to see includes:

x = 10
y = 0
result = 0
try:
    result = x/y
    print(result)
except ZeroDivisionError:
    print ("You are trying to divide by zero.")

Take a look at the two codes above. The one that we just did looks a little bit similar to the one above it, but this one has a message inside. This message is going to show up when the user raises this particular exception. You won't get the string of letters and numbers that don't make sense, and with this one, the user will know exactly what has gone wrong and can fix that error.

Can I define my own exceptions?

In the examples above, we took some time to define and handle the exceptions that the compiler offered to us and are already found in the Python library. Now it is time for us to take it a bit further and learn how to raise a few of our own exceptions in any kind of code that we want to write. Maybe you are working on a code that only allows for a few choices to the user, one that only allows them to pick certain numbers or one that only allows them to have so many chances at guessing. These are common things that we see when we work with gaming programs but can work well in other programs that you design.

When you make these kinds of exceptions, the compiler is going to have to be told that an exception is being raised, because it is not going to see that there is anything wrong in this part of the code. The programmer has to go in and let the compiler know what rules it has to follow, and what exceptions need to be raised in the process. A good example of the syntax that you can use to make this happen in your own code will be below:

class CustomException(Exception):
def_init_(self, value):
    self.parameter = value
def_str_(self):
    return repr(self.parameter)

try:
    raise CustomException("This is a CustomError!")
except CustomException as ex:
    print("Caught:", ex.parameter)

In this code, you have been successful in setting up your own exceptions and whenever the user raises one of these exceptions, the message of "Caught: This is a CustomError!" is going to come up on the screen. This is the best way to show your users that you have added in a customer exception into the program, especially if this is just one that you personally created for this part of the code, and not one that the compiler is going to recognize on its own.

Just like with the other examples that we went through, we worked with some generic wording just to show how exceptions are able to work. You can easily go through and change this up so that you get a message that is unique for the code that you are writing and will explain to the user what is going on when they get the error message to show up.

Learning how to work with some of the exceptions that can come up in your code is one of the best ways to make sure that your codes work the way that you want, that the user is going to like working with your program, and that everything is going to proceed as normal and do what you want. Take some time to practice these examples and see how they can work for you in order to handle any of the exceptions that come up in your code.

Chapter 9: Data Analysis with Python

Another topic that we need to explore a bit here is how Python, and some of the libraries that come with it, can work with the process of data analysis. This is an important process for any businesses because it allows them to take all of the data and information they have been collecting for a long time, and then can put it to good use once they understand what has been said within the information. It can be hard for a person to go through all of this information and figure out what is there, but for a data analyst who is able to use Python to complete the process, it is easy to find the information and the trends that you need.

The first thing that we need to look at here though is what data analysis is all about. Data analysis is going to be the process that companies can use in order to extract out useful, relevant, and even meaningful information from the data they collect, in a manner that is systematic. This ensures that they are able to get the full information out of everything and see some great results in the process. There are a number of reasons that a company would choose to work on their own data analysis, and this can include:

1. Parameter estimation, which helps them to infer some of the unknowns that they are dealing with.
2. Model development and prediction. This is going to be a lot of forecasting in the mix.
3. Feature extraction which means that we are going to identify some of the patterns that are there.
4. Hypothesis testing. This is going to allow us to verify the information and trends that we have found.
5. Fault detection. This is going to be the monitoring of the process that you are working on to make sure that there aren't any biases that happen in the information.

One thing that we need to make sure that we are watching out for is the idea of bias in the information that we have. If you go into the data analysis with the idea that something should turn out a certain way, or that you are going to manipulate the data so it fits the ideas that you have, there are going to be some problems. You can always change the data to say what you would like, but this doesn't mean that you are getting the true trends that come with this information, and you may be missing out on some of the things that you actually need to know about.

This is why a lot of data analysts will start this without any kind of hypothesis at all. This allows them to see the actual trends that come with this, and then see where the information is going to take you, without any kind of slant with the information that you have. This can make life easier and ensures that you are actually able to see what is truly in the information, rather than what you would like to see in that information.

Now, there are going to be a few different types of data that you can work with. First, there is going to be the deterministic. This is going to also be known as the data analysis that is non-random. And then there is going to be the stochastic, which is pretty much any kind that is not going to fit into the category of deterministic.

The Data Life Cycle

As we go through this information, it is important to understand some of the different phases that come with the data life cycle. Each of these comes together to ensure that we are able to understand the information that is presented to us and that we are able to use all of the data in the most efficient and best way possible.

There are a few stages that are going to come with this data life cycle, and we are going to start out with some of the basics to discuss each one to help us see what we are able to do with the data available to us. First, we work with data capture. The first experience that an individual or a company should have with a data item is to have it pass through the firewalls of the enterprise. This is going to be known as the Data Capture, which is basically going to be the act of creating values of data that do not exist yet and have never actually existed in that enterprise either. There are three ways that you can capture the data including:

1. Data acquisition: This is going to be the ingestion of data that is already existing that was produced by the organization but outside of the chosen enterprise.
2. Data entry: This is when we are dealing with the creation of new data values to help with the enterprise and it is done by devices or human operators that can help to generate the data needed.
3. Signal reception: This is where we are going to capture the data that a device has created with us, typically in the control system, but can be found in the Internet of Things if we would like.

The next part is going to be known as Data Maintenance. This is going to be where you supply the data to points at which data synthesis and data usage can occur in the next few steps. And it is best if you are able to work out the points so that they are going to be ready to go in this kind of phase.

What we will see during the data maintenance is that we are working to process the data, without really working to derive any value out of it yet. This is going to include integration changed data, cleansing, and making sure that the data is in the right format and as complete as possible before we get started. This ensures that no matter what method or algorithm you choose to work with here, you are going to be able to have the data ready to go.

Once you have been able to maintain the data and get it all cleaned up, it is time to work on the part known as data synthesis. This is a newer phase in the cycle and there are some places where you may not see this happen. This is going to be where we create some of the values of data through inductive logic and using some of the data that we have from somewhere else as the input. The data synthesis is going to be the arena of analytics that is going to use modeling of some kind to help you get the right results in the end.

Data usage comes next. This data usage is going to be the part of the process where we are going to apply the data as information to tasks that the enterprise needs to run and then handle the management on its own. This would be a task that normally falls outside of your life cycle for the data. However, data is becoming such a central part of the model for most businesses and having this part done can make a big difference.

For example, the data itself can be a service or a product, or at least part of this service or product. This would then make it a part of the data usage as well. The usage of the data is going to have some special challenges when it comes to data governance. One of these is whether it is legal to use the data in the ways that most people in business would like. There could be some issues like contractual or regulatory constraints on how we can use this data and it is important that these are maintained as much as possible.

Once we have figured out the data usage, it is time to move on to data publication. In being used, it may be possible that our single data value may be sent outside of the enterprise. This is going to be known as the data publication, which we can define as the sending of data to a location that is not within the enterprise.

A good example of this would be when you have a brokerage that sends out some monthly statements to their client. Once the data has been sent outside the enterprise, it is de facto impossible to get that information back. When the values of data are wrong and you publish it, it is impossible to correct them because they are now beyond the reach of your enterprise. The idea of Data Governance, like we talked about before, is going to have to handle how this information that is incorrect can be handled with.

Next on the list is the data archival. We will see that the single data value that we are working with can sometimes experience a lot of different rounds of usage and then publication, but eventually, it is going to reach the very end of its life. The first part of this means that we need to be able to take the value of the data and archive it. When we work on the process of Data Archival, it is going to mean that we are copying the data to an environment where it is stored in case we need it again, in an active production environment, and then we will remove the data from all of those active environments as well.

This kind of archive for the data is simply going to be a place where the data is stored, but where no publication, usage, or maintenance is going to happen. If necessary, it is possible to take any of the data that is in the archive and bring it back out to use again.

And finally, we reach the part of data purging. This is going to be the end that comes with our single data value and the life cycle that it has gone through. Data purging is going to be when we remove every copy of data from the enterprise. If possible, you will reach this information through the archive. If there is a challenge from Data Governance at this point, it is just there to prove that the information and the data have gone through the proper purging procedure at that time.

Working with data analysis and why it is important

With this in mind, we need to pay attention to why we would want to work on data analysis to start with? Do we really need to be able to look through all of this information to find the trends, or is there another method? Let's look at an example of what can happen when we do this data analysis and why you would want to use it.

Let's consider that we are looking at a set of data that includes information about the weather that occurred across the globe between the years 2015 to 2018. We are also going to have information that is base don the country between these years as well. So, there is going to be a percentage of ran within that country and we are going to have some data that concerns this in our set of data as well.

Now, what if you would like to go through all of that data, but you would like to only take a look at the data that comes with one specific country. Let's say that you would like to look at America and you want to see what percentage of rain it received between 2016 and 2017. Now, how are you going to get this information in a quick and efficient manner?

What we would need to do to make sure that we were able to get ahold of this particular set of data is to work with the data analysis. There are several algorithms, especially those that come from machine learning, that would help you to figure out the percentage of rain that America gets between 2016 to 2017. And this whole process is going to be known as what data analysis is really all about.

The Python Panda Library

When it comes to doing some data analysis in Python, the best extension that you can use is

Pandas. This is an open-sourced library that works well with Python and it is going to provide you with a high level of performance, data structures that are easy for even a beginner to use, and tools to make data analysis easy with Python. There are a lot of things to enjoy about this language, and if you want to be able to sort through all of the great information that you have available with the help of Python, then this is the library that you need to work with.

There are a lot of things that you can enjoy when it comes to working on the Python library. First off, this is one of the most popular and easy to use libraries when it comes to data science and it is going to work on top of the NumPy library. The name of Pandas that was given to this library is derived from the word of Panel Data, which is going to be an Econometrics from Multidimensional data. And one thing that a lot of coders are going to like about working with Pandas is that it is able to take a lot of the data that you need, including a SQL database or a TSV and CSV file, and will use it to create an object in Python.

This object is going to have columns as well as rows called the data frame, something that looks very similar to what we see with a table in statistical software including Excel.

There are many different features that are going to set Pandas apart from some of the other libraries that are out there. Some of the benefits that you are going to enjoy the most will include:

1. There are some data frames or data structures that are going to be high level compared to some of the others that you can use.
2. There is going to be a streamlined process in place to handle the tabular data, and then there is also a functionality that is rich for the time series that you want to work with.
3. There is going to be the benefit of data alignment, missing data-friendly statistics, merge, join, and groupby methods to help you handle the data that you have.
4. You are able to use the variety of structures for data in Pandas, and you will be able to

freely draw on the functions that are present in SciPy and NumPy to help make sure manipulation and other work can be done the way that you want.

Before we move on from here, we also need to have a good look at what some of the types of data are when it comes to Pandas. Pandas is going to be well suited when it comes to a large amount of data and will be able to help you sort through almost any kind of data that you would like. Some of the data types that are going to be the most suitable for working with the Pandas library with Python will include:

1. Any kind of tabular data that is going to have columns that are heterogeneously typed.
2. Arbitrary matrix data that has labels for the columns and rows.
3. Unordered and ordered time-series data
4. Any other kinds of sets of data that are statistical and observational.

Working with the Pandas library is one of the best ways to handle some of the Python codings that you want to do with the help of data analysis. As a company, it is so important to be able to go through and not just collect data, but also to be able to read through that information and learn some of the trends and the information that is available there. being able to do this can provide your company with some of the insights that it needs to do better, and really grow while providing customer service.

There are a lot of different methods that you can use when it comes to performing data analysis. And some of them are going to work in a different way than we may see with Python or with the Pandas library. But when it comes to efficiently and quickly working through a lot of data and having a multitude of algorithms and more that can sort through all of this information, working with the Python Pandas is the best option.

Chapter 10: Can I Test my Code?

As you are working on some of the codings that you would like to in Python, it is important that you stop on occasion and think about some of the steps that you can do to test out your code in Python. This is going to make sure that any code you have written out in Python is going to work the way that you want, and that there will not be any bugs that show up in the coding as well. We are going to spend some time in this chapter looking at how you can test out any codes that you are writing in Python, and how you can use this to your advantage to make your code strong and to make sure that it works properly.

Manual and Automated Testing

The good thing to consider here is that it is likely you have gone through and created a test without realizing it. Remember when you went through and ran your application and then made sure to use it for the first time? Did you stop here and test out the features and see if they were all working? This is known as a form of exploratory testing, and it is going to be considered a form of manual testing that you can use.

Exploratory testing is going to be a great way to learn more about a program and how it works. It is basically a type of testing that is going to be done without having a good solid plan in place. In this kind of test, you are not looking to get anything out of it or looking to see something specific happen. But you are just taking some time to open up your chosen application and poke around to see how things work.

To have a complete set of the manual tests, you have to make a list of all the different features that are available in the application, the different inputs that it is able to accept, and the results that you are expecting. Now, every time that you go through and try to make some changes to your code, it is time for you to go through every single item that is on that list, and double-check that it is working and doing what you want. Of course, this doesn't sound like a lot of fun and can make coding even more complicated for a beginner, which is why you may not use manual testing that much.

This is the place where we need to start talking more about automated testing. This kind of testing is going to be the execution of your test plan, which is the parts of the application that you wish to get tested, the order you want them tested in, and the expected responses you plan to get out of them, by a script rather than you or another programmer having to go through and do the work. Python is already going to provide us with some tools, as well as some libraries, to create the automated tests for your applications.

Integration Tests and Unit Tests

When we enter into the world of testing, there is going to be a lot of terminologies that happens around us. And now that you know a bit about manual testing and automated testing, and how they are different, it is time to take ourselves a bit deeper. Think about how you would go through and test the lights that are on your car. It is likely that you would turn on the lights, which is your test step, and either ask a friend to check or you would check on your own, whether the lights did turn on, and this is going to be the test assertion. Testing more than one component is going to be known as integration testing.

Think about all of the different parts that have to come together and work in the correct manner in order to make sure that even the simple task above is going to give you the results that you want. These components are going to be similar to what we see with all the parts that are in your application, all of the modules, functions, and classes that you have already been able to write.

One of the biggest challenges that you are going to face when doing an integration test is when it doesn't provide you with the results that you need.

It is hard to go through and provide a diagnosis to an issue without being able to go through and isolate out which part of the system is doing the failing. If the lights don't turn on, think about how many problems could be present that are causing that one issue. Maybe the bulb is broken, the computer of the car is failing, the alternator isn't working, or the battery could be dead.

Now, if you have a newer car that has a good computer in it, it is going to tell you when the light bulbs have gone out, saving you some time and hassle. It is going to do this with the help of a unit test. The unit test is going to be a smaller test, one that is going to be able to check that a single component operates in the way that you want. A unit test is going to help you to go through all of the problems and isolate what is broken inside that application, setting it to the side to fix later.

There are going to be two types of tests that fit in with this. The first one is going to be known as the integration test that will check the components of your application to see if they operate with each other. And then there is the unit test that is going to spend some time checking out the small components that come with your application. It is possible for you to write out both the unit tests and the integration tests with the help of Python.

One of the first things that you will need to do when running one of these tests in your code is to choose which test runner is the best for you. There are a lot of different test runners out there for you to choose from with Python. The one that is already found in the standard library for Python is going to be the unittest. We are going to use this in order to help us get the work done in the next few pages. The principles that come with this one is going to be portable with ease to other frameworks. The three most popular test runners are going to include some of the following:

1. Pytest
2. Nose or nose2
3. Unittest

Choosing the test runner that is going to be the right one for you is going to look at the things that you want to get done during the test, along with some of your level of experience in the process. But first, we are going to explore a bit more about the unittest and how it can work for you.

Unittest is something that has been around with Python for some time. in fact, it was built into the standard library that comes with Python back during Python 2.1 and has been a standard of that every sense. You will most likely see this in some of the commercial applications of Python, along with some of the projects that are open-sourced. Unittest is going to contain both a testing framework that you can use and a test runner. It also has some requirements that are important and that we need to follow when it comes to executing and writing the tests. These strict and important requirements for your tests with unittest are going to include:

1. You need to make sure that your tests are put into classes as a method.

2. You can use a series of assertion methods that are special in the unit test. Testcase class is sometimes one that is used rather than the built-in assert statement.

Then we need to make sure that we are using all of this in the proper manner as well. To make sure that we are able to convert an example that you may have already worked on, or worked on earlier, to the test case with unit test, you would need to use the following steps to get it done:

1. Import, from your standard library the unit test.
2. Create a new class that we are going to call TestSum. This is the one that will inherit everything from the TestCase class.
3. You can then move on to converting the test functions over into methods by adding self as the argument that is used first.
4. Then we can move on to changing up some of the assertions. We want to change this to self.assertEqual() inside the class known as TestCase.

5. And the final step that we need to work on is changing the entry point on the command line so that it calls up the unittest.main().

Now that we know a few of the instructions that we need to follow in order to run one of our own tests, it is time to look at some of the steps and the code that is needed to create a new file test_sum_Unittest.py. The code that we can use to make this happen includes:

import unittest

class TestSum(unittest.TestCase):

   def test_sum(self):
      self.assertEqual(sum([1, 2, 3]), 6, "Should be 6")

   def test_sum_tuple(self):
      self.assertEqual(sum((1, 2, 2)), 6, "Should be 6")

```
if __name__ == '__main__':
    unittest.main()
```

Before you try to write your own test though, we need to make sure that we know the right steps that are needed in order to structure one of these simple tests. Before you really try to dive into writing some of these tests, there are going to be a few decisions that you have to make. you need to first figure out what you would like to test. And then you need to figure out whether or not you are writing what is known as an integration test or a unit test. From here, you need to have the right kind of workflow in place to help get it all done. The loose schedule that you should follow with your workflow should include:

1. Create the inputs that you would like to use.
2. Execute the code that you are trying to test, making sure that you are able to capture the output that it gives.
3. Make sure that you compare the output against what result you were hoping to get.

If there are differences, it is time to explore why.

For this application, we are going to take some time to test out the function of sum(). There are many different kinds of behaviors that we can look for in this kind of function to see if it is working in a proper manner. We could check out whether it can sum a list of whole numbers, also known as integers, if it is able to sum out a set or a tuple, if it is able to sum out a list of floats, what is going to happen with the code if you provide it with a value that is seen as bad and what is going to happen when you use this and one of the values ends up being negative?

The simplest out of all these tests are going to be the one that is able to list out the integers. We are going to start this one out by creating our own file that has test.py in it. We are going to use the code below to help us get this done:

import unittest

```python
from my_sum import sum


class TestSum(unittest.TestCase):
    def test_list_int(self):
        """
        Test that it can sum a list of integers
        """
        data = [1, 2, 3]
        result = sum(data)
        self.assertEqual(result, 6)

if __name__ == '__main__':
    unittest.main()
```

There is a lot that goes on here in this code, and we are going to take a moment to look at it a bit closer. We see that it is going to be able to import the function of sum() from our package that we created earlier. Then it is going to define out a new test case class that we called TestSum, which is going to inherit the information from unittest.TestCase. It is also able to define the test method that we are using. In this one, we are working with test_list_int() in order to test out the different integers that we are working with. This allows us to declare a value that has data with a list of numbers, can help to assign the results of the my_sum.sum(data) to a result variable then it can assert that the value of result equals 6 by using the .assertEqual() method on your class.

Now, the last step that we need to use in order to write out a test is to make sure that we can validate the output we get against a known response. This is going to be the process of an assertion. There are going to be a few best practices that you are able to follow when it comes to writing your own assertions and these will include:

1. Make sure that any test you try to run is repeatable and then run the test more than one time in order to ensure it is going to provide you with the same kind of result and answer each time.
2. Try and assert results that are going to relate to the input data that you have, such as checking that the result is actually going

to be the sum of values in the sum() example.

Before we end this chapter, we need to take some time to look at a few of the side effects that come with writing our own tests. It is not always going to be as simple as it seems or as simple as looking back at some of the return value that comes with the function. Often, making sure that you can execute a piece of code is going to alter some of the other parts that happen in the environment, such as the attribute of a class, one of the files that are on the filesystem, or a value that should be in your database.

These issues are going to be known as the side effects, and they are definitely a big and important part when it comes to your testing. Deciding if the side effect is the part that is being tested or not before including it on your list of assertions can make a big difference in the kind of results that you would like to get, and whether they are going to turn out the way that you would like.

If you find that the unit of code that you are trying to test ends up with a ton of side effects, then it is possible that you are breaking the Single Responsibility Principle. This is basically going to mean that the part of the code that you are working on is already doing too much at once, and it is better for it to have everything refactored. Following this kind of principle is going to be one of the best ways that you can design out a code that is easy to write, repeatable, and simple to test for while still doing what you would like.

Testing is not always one of the best or most fun experiences when it comes to all of the codings that you can do. But it is definitely something that you need to add into the mix and that you need to focus on to ensure that your code is going to work in the manner that you want. When this is organized and ready to work, and you have been able to try out the testing at least a few times to make sure you get the right results, then you know your code is ready to use.

Chapter 11: Python and Artificial Intelligence

Artificial intelligence is something that is taking over the world. Many projects are now relying on this kind of programming to help make sure that things line up the way that they should, and that the program is able to perform and think on its own. It is amazing what artificial intelligence is able to do, taking on more things than we would have been able to do in the past.

The first thing that we need to explore is the idea of artificial intelligence. We already spent some time on Python and some of the different things that you are able to do with the programming of this, so knowing how to add in some of this coding to artificial intelligence, and knowing more about what AI consists of can make a big difference.

First, artificial intelligence is going to be one of the many sub-fields that fit in with computer science. It has a goal of enabling the development of computers so that these machines are able to do the tasks that are often reserved for people. This could happen in particular things that involve a person acting in an intelligent manner. This was a term that a researcher from Stanford, John McCarthy, coined in 1956 during what is known today as The Dartmouth Conference and the core mission that comes with artificial intelligence was then defined.

If we are able to start out or exploration with this definition, then it is reasonable to think that any kind of program is considered AI if it does something that we would normally think of as intelligent in humans. The way that the program goes about doing this is not going to be the biggest issue. Just that the program is actually able to do this work. That is, it is AI if it is smart, but it doesn't have to necessarily be smart like us.

It turns out that each programmer is going to have their own goals when it comes to working on systems built on AI, and these are all going to really fall within three camps, based on how close the machines are building line up with how people behave and think.

For some, the whole goal of using AI is to build up a system that is able to think in the exact same manner that humans do, but usually in a faster and more efficient way. and then there are those programmers who just want to get the job done and they are not going to care of the computation has anything to do with the thoughts that humans have. And finally, there are some people in between who are going to use human reasoning as a model that can inform and inspire but not as the final target for imitation.

The work that is aimed at getting the system set up to simulate human reasoning tends to be known as strong AI. This is because any of the results can be used in order to not only build systems that think but are also able to help us explain how humans think as well. However, it is still something that we have not seen on a regular basis because it is a really hard problem for us to solve. When that time does come, and we start to see more of this in technology and in our daily lives, then it is going to be a big day and will make a big difference in what we are able to see in our lives.

Then the work that is able to fall into the second camp, the one that is aimed at just being able to get the system to work is going to be known as the weak AI. This means that while we might be able to build up a system that kind of behaves like a human does the results is not going to tell us anything about how a person is going to think. One example of this in work is the Deep Blue from IBM, a system that was a master chess player, but it was not able to play in a similar manner to humans.

And then there is the camp that is in between the strong and the weak AI and we are going to call this third came the in-between. These are the systems that are going to be inspired and otherwise informed by human reasoning. This tends to be where most of the more powerful work in AI and other forms of computer science is going on today. These systems are going to use the reasoning of humans as a guide, but they do not have the end goal to perfectly model it.

A good example of what falls into this third category is IBM Watson. This program builds up evidence for the answers that it is able to find simply by looking at thousands of different texts so that it gains a good amount of confidence in the conclusion that it has. It is going to combine the ability to recognize a pattern in the texts that it reads with the ability to weigh the evidence that matching those patterns provides.

The development that came with this kind of program was guided by the observations of how people are able to come to various conclusions without us having a set of rules that we have to follow, and instead it is going to build up a collection of evidence that helps to back it up. Just like how humans are able to do, Watson is going to be able to get to notice some of the patterns that are found in the text that provides a bit of evidence and then will add up all of the different parts that it has in order to get that answer.

In addition, some of the deep learning that has come with Google is going to have a similar kind of feel. We mean that it is going to be inspired by the structure that we actually see in the brain. Informed by the behavior of the neurons, the systems of deep learning are going to function by learning layers of representations for tasks including speech recognition and image recognition. This may not be exactly the same as the brain is going to do the work, but this is something that does inspire it a bit.

The thing that we need to remember and take away here is that in order to look at a system and consider it a part of AI, rather than just a really good program, is that it doesn't have to just work the way that we do exactly. It just needs to be a program that is smart and can do some of the things that we talked about in this chapter.

Another thing that we need to take a look at while we are on this target is the difference between general AI and narrow AI. There is the narrow AI system that is going to be designed to handle a specific task, and then there are the general AI that is meant to have the ability to reason on things in general. Sometimes, it is easy to get a bit confused by this distinction, and this can make us mistakenly interpret specific results in a specific area as somehow being able to scope across all of the intelligent behavior.

Systems that are able to recommend things to you based on what you have done on that site in the past are going to be different compared to the systems that are going to take a look at an image and recognize that. And both of these are going to be different from any kind of system that is able to make decisions based on the syntheses of evidence. These are all going to be examples of narrow AI in practice, but you do not want to generalize them to address all of the issues that can happen with an intelligent machine that is able to work on its own. They are all smart and can all work with artificial intelligence, but they all do different things.

Now that we know a bit more about what artificial intelligence is all about, it is time to take a look at why you would like to work with artificial intelligence and the Python language altogether. These are used to help you write some of the programs that you want and can make a complicated task like artificial intelligence and make it as easy as possible.

There are a number of different benefits that are going to come with using Python as part of your plan with artificial intelligence. Whether you are a startup or a bigger company, you will find that Python is going to be able to provide a huge list of benefits to all. Using this language is such that it should not be limited to just one activity and it is growing popularity has allowed it to enter into things like natural language processing, artificial intelligence, data science, and machine learning.

But then this brings us some questions as well. How is Python is able to gain such momentum in AI and why would we want to work with this kind of language to help us to really work on some of this part of computer science, rather than using another kind of coding language to get this done. There are a lot of benefits to using Python to help you to work with machine learning and artificial intelligence, and some of these benefits include:

You can use less code. AI is going to involve a ton of code and a lot of algorithms to help make up that code. This is how you get the program to learn and act in the manner that you would like. You will find that adding Python into the mix can help to ease some of the testing, and even keep the lines of code needed for each algorithm down to a minimum. Python is going to be able to make the writing as well as the execution of the codes as simple as possible, it is able to implement the same logic with as much as $1/5^{th}$ of the code compared to many of the other coding languages that you want to use. And because of the interpreted approach that comes with it, you will be able to get some of the artificial intelligence work that you want to be done without having to write out as much confusing code to get it done.

The next benefit that comes with using the Python language when you want to work on artificial intelligence is all of the prebuilt libraries. Python is going to have a ton of different libraries that are going to help you with all of the projects that you want to do in AI. There are a few different ones that you can work with including Scikit-Learn, SciPy, NumPy and more. Python implementation of algorithms are going to be some of the best, and you are going to be able to pull them out of a lot of the libraries that you can find available through Python already. Having these dedicated libraries is going to save you a lot of time compared to coding on items that are still at the base level.

And then we can move on to the support that you will receive with this kind of coding, even when you are working on AI. Python is an open-sourced program that has an amazing community present. There is a ton of resources that are available which will ensure that any developer is up to speed on what they need to know in no time. there is also a big community of active coders who are willing to answer questions and help programmers no matter which stage they may be in when it comes to the cycle of developing.

The platform agnostics is important. Python is going to provide us with the flexibility to provide an API from an existing language which is going to make sure that we are able to get the work done. If it is also a platform-independent that is going to help us to get things done. With just a few changes in codes, you are going to get your app up and running in a new operating system. This is going to save the developers a lot of time when it comes to testing on all of the different platforms and migrating code the way that you would like. This makes it easier to use the AI that you are developing with Python on more than one platform, even if you are not going through and testing each of them.

Of course, Python is going to provide us with a good deal of flexibility, no matter what kind of code that we are working on. Flexibility is going to be a big advantage that comes with working on the Python code. With the option to choose between the scripting and the approach that is used with this language, Python is going to be so great no matter which program you are working with. It is also going to work as a good backend, and it is suitable for helping out with almost any kind of data structure and linking them all together in the process. The option to check a majority of the code in the IDE on its own is going to be another big plus for developers who are struggling with some of the algorithms that come with this kind of program

And the final benefit of working with the Python language with artificial intelligence is that it is really popular. Right now, Python is already being able to win the heart of many new programmers who are coming into the market and trying to make their mark with their own codes. Though AI projects need a very experienced programmer to get them done, it is possible to use Python in order to smoothen up some of the learning curves. It is so much easier for us to look for developers in Python than it is for programmers in different languages, especially in some different parts of the world depending on where you are looking.

There is just so much to love about using the Python language, and this has taken the world by storm, helping us find a lot of different programs and programmers that use Python. Add in the active community and some of the extended libraries along with some of the ever developing and improving code, and you can see why Python has turned into one of the most used languages in coding to work with today.

It is possible that some of the projects that you are going to work with over time can get a bit tricky. This is where using Python and some of the libraries that come with this are going to become handy and can be a good thing. In our last chapter, we are going to explore not only some exercises that you are able to do with Python in particular, but also some that you can do with machine learning and artificial intelligence to help you really explore what is available and see just how much easier the Python language can make some of the more complicated coding tasks.

Chapter 12: Python and Machine Learning

The final topic that we need to spend some time on is the idea of machine learning and how Python is going to be able to work along with this idea. Machine learning is going to be a type of artificial intelligence that is going to help us to really work on some of the different types of learning that a system is able to do. This one goes a bit more specifically into this kind of learning than we are going to see with artificial intelligence, and Python, along with a lot of the libraries that come with it, can help us to get the work done as easily as possible in your coding.

This kind of learning process is going to be helpful when it is time to start with observations, also known as data, like instructions, direct experience, surveys, examples, and more in order to figure out what trends and patterns are found in the data. Then the predictions that are pulled out of this data are used to help us know what is going to happen in the future. One of the main goals that is going to happen when we work with machine learning is that it will ensure that the computer is going to learn in a manner that is more automatic, meaning that it is able to learn how to do things without the help of a person or any programming coming in and making the adjustments here.

When you work with machine learning, you will find that it makes analyzing large quantities of data easier than ever. Machine learning can give us some results that are profitable, but of course, you first have to learn how to set it up, and there are a few resources that are needed before you are able to make this all happen. This type of coding is often going to take a bit more time to work with because you are basically training the models of machine learning to do what you want, even when you aren't there, which can really increase how much the system can do.

There are a lot of different things that you are able to use machine learning. Any time that you aren't sure how the end result is going to turn up, or you aren't sure what the input of the other person could be, you will find that machine learning can help you get through some of these problems. If you want the computer to be able to go through a long list of options and find patterns or find the right result, then machine learning is going to work the best for you. Some of the other things that machine learning can help out with include:

1. Being able to recognize the voice of someone
2. Being able to recognize the facial features of someone
3. The use of a search engine. You will find that the program here is going to be able to learn based on the answers that the user has put in, or the queries that they are searching for. Over time, the search engine will know more about what the user is looking for and can learn how to provide the best results over time.
4. As you are shopping, you may notice that there are recommendations that show up on the system as you go. These

recommendation channels are an example of machine learning.

5. Doing the data analysis that we talked about earlier. The machine learning process is going be able to sort through a lot of data about customers and finances and can make some good predictions about what a company should consider doing in order to increase how many happy customers and profits they can make along the way.

Of course, these are just a few of the more well-known examples that are out there when it comes to machine learning and trying to get the computer to figure out the right course of action to take on its own. Many of the programs that you are going to learn how to code with, including some of the ones that are in this guidebook, are going to be a bit easier to handle than this. They are going to be there, telling the computer exactly how it should behave and what it is going to do in each situation. But when it comes to working on machine learning and other parts of artificial intelligence, this is not going to be enough to see results.

When we go through some of the traditional codings that we have talked about in this guidebook, you will need to figure out, or at least try as much as you can, to limit how many choices your user is going to get to use. And then you would add in the catch-all to the program in order to make sure you didn't miss something. This works well for a lot of the programs that you want to write, but you can imagine that this is going to be falling short in some areas based on what you want to accomplish.

With machine learning, we need to work with a program that is able to adapt and change. We need to have a type of coding that is going to look at a problem and then figure out how it can learn from it and do what the user wants, in ways that traditional programming can't do. And this is where Python is going to be able to get into the mix and help us get the work done.

But first, we need to explore that there are three main types of machine learning algorithms that can be used. Each of these is going to work in a slightly different manner, but they can all be useful based on the kind of program that you want to write out and what needs to happen in the end. The three types of machine learning that you can work with include supervised machine learning, reinforcement machine learning, and unsupervised machine learning.

First, we will look at the supervised machine learning. This is when the programmer is going to feed in a lot of different examples to the code, in the hopes that when the algorithm works properly, the code is going to have a good idea of the rules and how to follow them. Taking the examples that it learned, the program will be able to make accurate predictions and function as it should. It is possible that there will still be some mistakes in the process, but it will learn how to do better with more examples over time, and you will find that it becomes pretty accurate pretty quickly.

Then we can move on to the unsupervised machine learning. This is going to be where the program is just going to learn on its own, based on the actions of the user and without needing all of the examples that the other type of learning is going to provide. This is something that we see with voice recognition. There is no way that the programmer would be able to go in and give enough examples to handle this. Instead, the program just learns how to recognize different words, and the dialects and the different speech patterns and then it gets better at this over time.

And finally, we reach the reinforcement machine learning. This one is similar to what we are going to see with the unsupervised machine learning, but it is going to rely more on the idea of true and false. The more that the program is able to get true, the stronger it can become. But when it makes mistakes, it can remember that as well and will look for a better path the next time around.

From here, we need to take a look at the Python language and how it is going to work inside the codes that you want to write as well. There are other languages that are going to work pretty well when you do machine learning, but none offer as many libraries, the power, the speed, and even the ease of use as you are going to get when you decide to add in some Python coding to any machine learning project that you would like to do.

While we will take a look at Python and how it works in a bit, it is important to note that Python is one of the best languages to work with when it comes to machine learning. Python is a simple language, one that is easy enough for beginners to the world of programming to work with. Yet it still has enough power behind it to make sure that you can still get some of the intense codes done that you would like. The language has a large library, works well with other coding languages if you decide to implement them together, and it is easy enough to read, even if you don't have any kind of coding practice or experience in the past.

Many of the codes and the different parts of the coding language that we discussed in this guidebook are going to be helpful even when you work with machine learning and some of the more complicated tasks that we will need to handle with machine learning. We will look in the next chapter at one of the machine learning algorithms that you are able to do with Python and you will see that while the code may be a bit longer than some of the others we have discussed, it is still pretty simple to work with and will include a lot of the parts you are already familiar with.

There is just so much that you are going to be able to do when it comes to working with machine learning, and when it is combined with the Python coding language, as well as with artificial intelligence and data analysis like we talked about through this guidebook, you will find that there is just so much that you can do, even with the beginner programming that we discussed in this guidebook!

Chapter 13: Practical Codes and Exercises to Use Python

Now that we have had some time to learn how to work with the Python code, it is time to take a look at some practical examples of working with this kind of coding language. We will do a few different Python exercises here so that you can have a little bit of fun and get a better idea of how you would use the different topics that we have talked about in this guidebook to your benefit. There are a lot of neat programs that you are able to use when you write in Python, but the ones in this chapter will give you a good idea of how to write codes, and how to use the examples that we talked about in this guidebook in real coding. So let's get started!

Creating a Magic 8 Ball

The first project that we are going to take a look at here is how to create your own Magic 8 ball. This will work just like a regular magic 8 ball, but it will be on the computer. You can choose how many answers that you would like to have available to those who are using the program but we are going to focus on having eight responses show up for the user at a random order so they get something different each time.

Setting up this code is easier than you think. Take some time to study this code, and then write it out into the compiler. See how many of the different topics we discussed in this guidebook show up in this code as well. The code that you need to use in order to create a program that includes your own Magic 8 ball will include:

 # Import the modules
import sys
import random

ans = True

while ans:
    question = raw_input("Ask the magic 8 ball a question: (press enter to quit)")

```
answers = random.randint(1,8)

if question == ""
    sys.exit()

elif answers ==1:
    print("It is certain")

elif answers == 2:
    print("Outlook good")

elif answers == 3:
print("You may rely on it")

elif answers == 4:
    print("Ask again later")

elif answers == 5:
    print("Concentrate and ask again")

elif answers == 6:
    print("Reply hazy, try again.")

elif answers == 7:
```

    print("My reply is no")

elif answers == 8:
    print("My sources say no")

Remember in this program, we chose to go with eight options because it is a Magic 8 ball and that makes the most sense. But if you would like to add in some more options, or work on another program that is similar and has more options, then you would just need to keep adding in more of the elif statement to get it done. This is still a good example of how to use the elif statement that we talked about earlier and can give us some good practice on how to use it. You can also experiment a bit with the program to see how well it works and make any changes that you think are necessary to help you get the best results.

How to make a Hangman Game

The next project that we are going to take a look at is creating your own Hangman game. This is a great game to create because it has a lot of the different options that we have talked about throughout this guidebook and can be a great way to get some practice on the various topics that we have looked at. We are going to see things like a loop present, some comments, and more and this is a good way to work with some of the conditional statements that show up as well.

Now, you may be looking at this topic and thinking it is going to be really hard to work with a Hangman game. It is going to have a lot of parts that go together as the person makes a guess and the program tries to figure out what is going on, whether the guesses are right, and how many chances the user gets to make these guesses. But using a lot of the different parts that we have already talked about in this guidebook can help us to write out this code without any problems. The code that you need to use in order to create your very own Hangman game in Python includes:

 # importing the time module
importing time

```
#welcoming the user
Name = raw_input("What is your name?")

print("Hello, + name, "Time to play hangman!")

print("
"

#wait for 1 second
time.sleep(1)

print("Start guessing...")
time.sleep(.05)

#here we set the secret
word = "secret"

#creates a variable with an empty value
guesses = ' '

#determine the number of turns
turns = 10

#create a while loop
```

#check if the turns are more than zero
while turns > 0:

    #make a counter that starts with zero
    failed = 0

    #for every character in secret_word
    for car in word:
    #see if the character is in the players guess
    if char in guesses:

    #print then out the character
    print char,

    else

    # if not found, print a dash
    print "_",

    # and increase the failed counter with one
    failed += 1

    #if failed is equal to zero

```
#print You Won
if failed == 0:
    print("You Won")

#exit the script
    Break

print

# ask the user go guess a character
guess = raw_input("guess a character:")

#set the players guess to guesses
guesses += guess

# if the guess is not found in the secret word
if guess not in word:

    #turns counter decreases with 1 (now 9)
    turns -= 1

    #print wrong
```

print("Wrong")

 # how many turns are left
Print("You have," + turns, 'more guesses')

#if the turns are equal to zero
if turns == 0

#print "You Loose"

Okay, so yes, this is a longer piece of code, especially when it is compared to the Magic 8 Ball that we did above, but take a deep breath, and go through it all to see what you recognize is there. This isn't as bad as it looks, and much of it is actually comments to help us see what is going on at some of the different parts of the code. This makes it easier to use for our own needs and can ensure that we know what is going on in the different parts. There are probably a lot of other things that show up in this code that you can look over and recognize that we talked about earlier as well. This makes it easier for you to get the code done!

Making your own K-means algorithm

Now that we have had some time to look at a few fun games and examples that you are able to do with the help of the Python code, let's take a moment to look at some of the things that you can do with machine learning and artificial intelligence with your coding. We spent some time talking about how you can work with these and some of the different parts of the code, as well as how Python is going to work with the idea of machine learning. And now we are going to take that information and create one of our own machine learning algorithms to work with as well.

Before we work on a code for this one, we need to take a look at what this k-means clustering means. This is a basic algorithm that works well with machine learning and is going to help you to gather up all of the data that you have in your system, the data that isn't labeled at the time, and then puts them all together in their own little group of a cluster.

The idea of working with this kind of cluster is that the objects that fall within the same cluster, whether there are just two or more, are going to be related to each other in some manner or another, and they are not going to be that similar to the data points that fall into the other clusters. The similarity here is going to be the metric that you will want to use in order to show us the strength that is in the relationship between the two.

When you work on this particular algorithm, it is going to be able to form some of the clusters that you need of the data, based on how similar the values of data that you have. You will need to go through and give them a specific value for K, which will be how many clusters that you would like to use. It is best to have at least two, but the number of these clusters that you work with will depend on how much data you have and how many will fit in with the type of data that you are working with.

With this information in mind and a good background of what the K-means algorithm is going to be used for, it is time to explore a bit more about how to write your own codes and do an example that works with K-means. This helps us to practice a bit with machine learning and gives us a chance to practice some of our own new Python skills.

```
import numpy as np
import matplotlib.pyplot as plt


def d(u, v):
    diff = u - v
    return diff.dot(diff)


def cost(X, R, M):
    cost = 0
    for k in xrange(len(M)):
        for n in xrange(len(X)):
            cost += R[n,k]*d(M[k], X[n])
    return cost
```

After this part, we are going to take the time to define your function so that it is able to run the k-means algorithm before plotting the result. This is going to end up with a scatterplot where the color will represent how much of the membership is inside of a particular cluster. We would do that with the following code.

```
def plot_k_means(X, K, max_iter=20, beta=1.0):
    N, D = X.shape
    M = np.zeros((K, D))
    R = np.ones((N, K)) / K

    # initialize M to random
    for k in xrange(K):
        M[k] = X[np.random.choice(N)]

    grid_width = 5
    grid_height = max_iter / grid_width
    random_colors = np.random.random((K, 3))
    plt.figure()
```

```
costs = np.zeros(max_iter)
for i in xrange(max_iter):
    # moved the plot inside the for loop
    colors = R.dot(random_colors)
    plt.subplot(grid_width, grid_height, i+1)
    plt.scatter(X[:,0], X[:,1], c=colors)

    # step 1: determine assignments / responsibilities
    # is this inefficient?
    for k in xrange(K):
        for n in xrange(N):
            R[n,k] = np.exp(-beta*d(M[k], X[n])) / np.sum( np.exp(-beta*d(M[j], X[n])) for j in xrange(K) )

    # step 2: recalculate means
    for k in xrange(K):
        M[k] = R[:,k].dot(X) / R[:,k].sum()

    costs[i] = cost(X, R, M)
    if i > 0:
        if np.abs(costs[i] - costs[i-1]) < 10e-5:
```

break

plt.show()

Notice here that both the M and the R are going to be matrices. The R is going to become the matrix because it holds onto 2 indices, the k and the n. M is also a matrix because it is going to contain the K individual D-dimensional vectors. The beta variable is going to control how fuzzy or spread out the cluster memberships are and will be known as the hyperparameter. From here, we are going to create a main function that will create random clusters and then call up the functions that we have already defined above.

def main():
  # assume 3 means
  D = 2 # so we can visualize it more easily
  s = 4 # separation so we can control how far apart the means are
  mu1 = np.array([0, 0])
  mu2 = np.array([s, s])

```python
mu3 = np.array([0, s])


N = 900 # number of samples
X = np.zeros((N, D))
X[:300, :] = np.random.randn(300, D) + mu1
X[300:600, :] = np.random.randn(300, D) + mu2
X[600:, :] = np.random.randn(300, D) + mu3

# what does it look like without clustering?
plt.scatter(X[:,0], X[:,1])
plt.show()


K = 3 # luckily, we already know this
plot_k_means(X, K)


# K = 5 # what happens if we choose a "bad" K?
# plot_k_means(X, K, max_iter=30)

# K = 5 # what happens if we change beta?
# plot_k_means(X, K, max_iter=30, beta=0.3)


if __name__ == '__main__':
```

main()

Yes, this process is going to take some time to write out here, and it is not always an easy process when it comes to working through the different parts that come with machine learning and how it can affect your code. But when you are done, you will be able to import some of the data that your company has been collecting, and then determine how this compares using the K-means algorithm as well.

Conclusion

Thank for making it through to the end of Python *for Beginners*. Let's hope it was informative and able to provide you with all of the tools you need to achieve your goals whatever they may be.

The next step is to take some time to look at the different examples that we have explored in this guidebook and use these to help you learn more about how to work with the Python language, and some of the neat things that you are able to do with this coding language. There are a lot of other coding languages out there that you are able to work with, but Python is one of the best that works for most beginner programmers, providing the power and the ease of use that you are looking for when you first get started in this kind of coding language. This guidebook took the time to explore how Python works, along with some of the different types of coding that you can do with it.

In addition to seeing a lot of examples of how you can code in Python and how you can create some of your own programs in this language, we also spent some time looking at how to work with Python when it comes to the world of machine learning, artificial intelligence, and data analysis. These are topics and parts of technology that are taking off and many programmers are trying to learn more about. And with the help of this guidebook, you will be able to handle all of these, even as a beginner in Python.

When you are ready to learn more about how to work with the Python coding language and how you are able to make sure that you can even use Python along with data analysis, artificial intelligence, and machine learning, make sure to check out this guidebook to help you get started.

Finally, if you found this book useful in any way, a review on Amazon is always appreciated!

Python Programming

The Crash Course for Python – Learn the Secrets of Machine Learning, Data Science Analysis and Artificial intelligence. Introduction to Deep Learning for beginners

Table of Contents

Introduction

Chapter 1: What is Deep Learning and Artificial Intelligence

Chapter 2: A Look at Machine Learning

Chapter 3: An Introduction to Python

Chapter 4: The Scikit-Learn Library

Chapter 5: Creating a Neural Network with Scikit-Learn

Chapter 6: The TensorFlow Library

Chapter 7: K-Nearest Neighbors and K-Means Clustering

Chapter 8: Decision Trees and Random Forests in Machine Learning

Chapter 9: The Linear Classifier and What This Means

Chapter 10: Are Recurrent Neural Networks Different From Neural Networks

Chapter 11: What Else Can I Do with Python Programming and Machine Learning?

Conclusion

Introduction

The following chapters will discuss everything that you need to know in order to get started with Python programming. There may be many different options out there that you can choose from when it comes to coding your programs, but none of them can offer you the versatility, and all of the benefits, that you are going to be able to get with Python, and that is exactly what we are going to discuss when we are in this guidebook.

To start this guidebook, we are going to take a look at a few different topics that are ever more increasingly being discussed in relation to Python. We will spend a few chapters looking at artificial intelligence and deep learning, as well as taking in some information about machine learning before starting our own introduction into the Python language and what it is all about.

After this kind of introduction, it is time to start diving into all of the cool things that Python is able to do with machine learning and deep learning, and what better way to do this than taking a look at some of the different libraries of Python that were designed to work with this topic. We will spend some time looking at the Scikit-Learn library, how to create some neural networks with this library, and the TensorFlow library as well.

To finish this guidebook, we are going to spend our time taking a look at a few of the different algorithms that work with machine learning, and how you can use Python to help you write the codes that are needed to make those algorithms work. Some of the best machine learning algorithms that we are going to explore will include the K-Means clustering, K-Nearest Neighbors, Decision Trees, Linear Classifiers and more.

Machine learning and artificial intelligence are becoming like big buzzwords in the industry, and many people are interested in learning how to use them for their own needs and their own kind of programming. While this is a great thing, many of these same people worry that these topics are going to be too hard to learn and to understand. With the help of the information in this guidebook, you will be able to really work on all of this, even as a beginner, with the help of Python. When you are ready to learn how to do some Python programming, and how it can work with machine learning, deep learning, and artificial intelligence, make sure to check out this guidebook to help you get started!

There are plenty of books on this subject on the market, thanks again for choosing this one! Every effort was made to ensure it is full of as much useful information as possible, please enjoy!

Chapter 1: What is Deep Learning and Artificial Intelligence

There are a lot of different parts that can come with coding and working with computers in our modern world. Many people feel that if they don't know how to do a complicated kind of coding, then they are not going to be able to do any at all. But this is just not true. There are many complex types of programming that you are able to do, and they are easier to complete than you may think. And in tis guidebook, we are going to take some of our time to discuss many of them.

To start out with in this chapter, we are going to take a look at deep learning and artificial intelligence. Both of these are going to be integral parts when we are looking at some of the topics that are in this guidebook, and knowing how to make them work, and what all we are able to do with them can make a difference in our coding and what we are able to do in the process. Some of the things that we need to know concerning deep learning and artificial intelligence will include the following:

What is deep learning

The first topic that we are going to spend some time on in this chapter is going to be deep learning. Deep learning is actually a type of machine learning (we will discuss more about that in the next chapter), that is going to be responsible for training our computer how to perform some of the life tasks that humans do. There are a variety of tasks that could fall into this category, but things like recognizing speech, identifying what is inside a picture, and making predictions can all fit into this idea.

Instead of organizing the data to run through equations that are already defined, deep learning is going to set up some of the basic parameters that you need for the data, and then will train the computer to learn on its own by being able to see the patterns through many different layers of processing.

Let's dive into this a bit more. Deep learning is important here because it is going to be a foundation of AI, or artificial intelligence, and the current interest that we are seeing in this deep learning is due to how it is related to AI. Deep learning and some of the techniques that come with it have been able to improve the ability of machines to describe, detect, recognize, and classify things in a way that was previously thought to only work for humans.

A good example of this is all of the different things that deep learning is already able to do in our world. We can find that many of the algorithms and techniques that work with it are great at describing the content that it is going to look through, at detecting objects, and recognizing the speech patterns of those using it, while recognizing what is inside one of the images that you present to it. There are many pieces of technology that use this, such as fraud detection, facial recognition, and systems like Cortana and Siri to name a few.

There are already a few developments who are working on advancing what we see with deep learning. Some of these are going to include:

1. The improvements that have been done on some of the algorithms have been able to boost up some of the methods that we see with deep learning.
2. There are some newer approaches to deep learning that have ensured that the accuracy of the models is going to stay intact.
3. There are even some neural networks that have new classes that are developed to fit well for some new applications, including the classification of images and the translation of text.
4. There is a ton of information available from companies, much more than was there in the past. This helps us to build up some new neural networks with a lot of deep layers,

including streaming data, physicians' notes, investigative transcripts, and even some textual data that you could get from social media.

5. There are also some computational advances of distributed cloud computing and graphics processing units which can give us all of the computing power that is needed in order to make sure the algorithms for deep learning can actually be done.

At the same time that all of that is going on, the human to machine interface that we are used to seeing is changing quite a bit as well. The keyboard and the mouse that were traditionally used are now being replaced with things like natural language, touch, gesture, and swipe. This opens up the field to even more AI and deep learning along the way.

This brings up the question of how deep learning can provide us with a lot of opportunities and applications in the process. A lot of power computationally is going to be needed in order to solve some of the deep learning problems, simply because the nature of iterations in these algorithms. This results in the complexity going up as the layers increase as well. And you also need to be able to handle a ton of data at the same time in order to get the networks trained and ready to go.

The dynamic nature of the methods of deep learning, and their ability to always adapt and improve to some of the changes in the underlying information pattern, will present us with the information and opportunity that we need to introduce a bit more of the dynamic behavior that is needed into the analytics.

In addition, we can add in a lot more of the personalization that customers want when the analytics comes into play with deep learning. Another great opportunity here is to improve the performance and accuracy of applications where the neural network is not brand new but has been around for a longer period of time. through some better algorithms, and more power to compute, we are able to get the benefit of adding in more depth.

The next thing that we can focus on is some of the different ways that you are able to use deep learning to help your business grow and to create some of the great technology that is needed at the same time. To someone who is not all that familiar with how this technology works, it may seem like deep learning is going to be the research phase for computer science and you won't be able to use it that much. However, it is possible to bring in some deep learning in many practical manners to businesses, and it is possible that you are already using quite a few of them today and didn't even notice the technology that is there.

Some of the different ways that deep learning is being used today and how we can benefit from it as well will include:

Speech recognition. Pretty much every industry in our world has seen some sort of use when it comes to speech recognition. If you have ever asked a question to a device, including your phone, to get an answer, then you have used this. Other places like Skype, Xbox, Google Now, and more are using this as well. The deep learning part is brought in because it helps the system to be able to not only recognize when someone is talking to it, but also know what the person is saying or asking as well.

Natural language processing is another place where deep learning is going to come into play. Neural networks, which are going to be a big component of deep learning, and that we will discuss in more detail later on, have already been used to process and even analyze some written texts for a long time. A specialization that comes with text mining, this kind of technique can be used in other places to discover the patterns that are found in places like news reports, the notes that a physician writes out for later, the complaints from some customers, and even more.

Deep learning can also come into play to help out with recognizing images. One of the more practical applications of this is with automatic image captioning and description of the scenes that are going on. This could be used in a lot of different contexts. But one of these is going to be an example of law enforcement investigations to identify some of the criminal activities that are present in the thousands of photos that bystanders in a busy area have submitted. This is just one example though. A self-driving care could benefit from this kind of technology when it is able to use its camera in all angles to go in the right direction.

And the fourth application that we can discuss when it comes to deep learning, although not the last, is going to be the recommendation systems. There are a lot of different companies who are using this, but some common examples of how this would work include Netflix and Amazon. The point of this is to check what you may be the most interested in next, based on the behavior that you have done in the past. Deep learning is going to be used in order to enhance some of the recommendations that happen in environments that are more complex, such as music interests or your preferences of clothing, even when they occur across more than one platform.

There is so much that you are able to do with deep learning and the world of this kind of programming is bound to keep growing in the future. Understanding what it is all about and how it can work will make a big difference in the amount of success that you are going to see with it over time as well!

What is artificial intelligence

The next kind of topic that we are going to spend some time on is that of artificial intelligence. This is going to be a kind of area of computer science that is going to emphasize how we can create machines that are intelligent, ones that are able to work and react in a manner that is similar to how humans did. There are a lot of different activities that computers that hold onto the artificial intelligence technology are designed for, and these are going to include things like:

1. Planning
2. Problem solving
3. Learning
4. Speech recognition

One thing that we can remember when we are working with artificial intelligence is that it is a branch of computer science. In this particular branch, we are going to aim to create machines that are intelligent, ones that are able to learn and think on their own. In fact, this has become such a prevalent thing in our world that it is know an essential part of the technology industry and we are going to see it grow and take off more than ever before.

There has been a lot of research done on artificial intelligence, especially with how much it has risen in popularity over the last few years. This kind of research has been focused and turned into something that is more specialized and highly technical like nothing before. The core problems that come with artificial intelligence are going to be that we need to be able to program a computer for a lot of different traits, and to get it to behave and think in a manner that is almost the same, but faster and more efficient, than we see with a human.

This is going to be complicated, and many programmers, both newer and more advanced, are going to wonder how we are supposed to make this happen at all. And is it really something that we are able to focus on and do, or are we just wasting our time with all of this? You will find that artificial intelligence has really started to take the world by storm, not because it is just a neat theory, but because of all the neat things that it is able to do in the process.

Right now, there are a lot of different ways that artificial intelligence can be used. And some of the things that we are already able to train a computer to do with the help of this technology will include the following:

1. The ability to move and manipulate any of the objects that you would like.
2. Planning
3. Problem solving
4. Reasoning
5. Learning
6. Perception
7. Knowledge

One of the core parts that you are going to see with some of this research into Ai is knowledge. Machines are able to be trained to act and give off reactions that are like humans, but this is only going to happen if the computer is able to learn off an abundant amount of information that teaches them how the world works. This kind of programming needs to have a lot of information, as well as access to relations, categories, objects, and properties between all of the parts so that it can put this to good use and become more knowledgeable.

It is amazing what all of this is able to do if we can work with the technology in the proper manner.

When the program or the machine is able to implement some of the artificial intelligence that we are talking about, it will be able to initiate things like common sense, it can start with reasoning and problem solving, and can handle tasks that are really hard to do and kind of tedious, in no time at all.

We are going to explore this in a bit more information below, but machine learning is also an important part that comes with AI. Learning without any supervision is going to require us to teach the computer how to identify patterns that come in quickly with our inputs, while learning with a lot of supervision means that the computer or the machine is going to be able to learn with the help of regression that is numerical and classification.

What does all this mean though? Classification is going to be important here because it is going to help us determine the category where one object is going to belong. And then the regression is going to help us deal with obtaining a set of numerical inputs or outputs to use as examples, which then helps us to discover functions enabling the generation of suitable outputs from the inputs that we are using.

As you can see, there are a lot of different components to talk about when it comes to deep learning and artificial intelligence and learning all of it will take a long time. but understanding some of the basics that we are talking about in this guidebook can help us to learn how these technologies are affecting our world, and even how we are able to use some of them for our own benefits as well.

Chapter 2: A Look at Machine Learning

The next topic that ewe need to spend some time exploring is the idea of machine learning. This is going to be a method of data analysis that is going to automate the analytical model building for us. It is going to fit in as one of the branches that comes with artificial intelligence because it is based on the idea that a system is able to learn from the data it receives, identify some of the different patterns that are there, and then make some decisions with a minimal amount of intervention from humans.

Because of a lot of the new technologies for computing that are available, machine learning has changed a lot in our modern world. It was born from pattern recognition and the theory that computers are able to learn without someone having to come in and program it to perform the tasks that you would like. The iterations that happen in machine learning are really important because as the models are given some more exposure to new data, they are going to be able to adapt independently. They will be able to learn from previous computations in order to produce reliable and repeatable decisions and results.

The system that is going to work with machine learning is able to learn from some of the previous computations that it went through in order to help it to get smarter. It is a type of science that is not going to necessarily be new, but it is going to be one that gains a lot of momentum in recent years.

While a lot of the algorithms out there for machine learning have been around for a very long time, the ability to automatically apply some of the mathematical calculations to the big data, at faster speeds and over and over again, is going to be a newer development. There are a lot of different applications that can come with machine learning, and this kind of technology is likely to take off steam in no time at all. Some of the most common applications that are out there that you are likely to have heard about and you may be more familiar with right now will include:

1. The self-driving car that is available through Google.
2. Online recommendation systems that we see from a lot of shopping systems like Amazon and some streaming services that you use like Netflix.
3. Knowing what the customers are saying about you on various social media accounts including Twitter.
4. Being able to detect what could potentially be fraud.

All of the new interest in machine learning is going to be due to some of the different factors that have been able to help you to do with data mining and have made this as well as the Bayesian analysis, even more popular than before. Things like the amount of data that is available, and how much and how many varieties are available than ever before. Add in that you will find that it is cheaper and more powerful and affordable to do computational processing and data storage that is affordable, it is no wonder that companies want to be able to work with the machine learning and some of the other parts that come with artificial intelligence and more.

All of these things may not mean much at first, but it does mean that it is possible to quickly and automatically produce models that are going to be able to go through a good analysis of bigger and more complex data and can deliver faster results that are more accurate than ever before. And machine learning can help you to do all of this on a scale that is much larger than ever before. And by being able to build up models that are precise, an organization is going to have a better chance of identifying some of the opportunities that are more profitable, or to avoid unknown risks that can show up.

There are going to be a few different things that need to be present in order to work with some of the systems of machine learning that will ensure they do what you would like. Some of these are going to include ensemble modeling, iterative and automation processes to get the work done, both basic and more advanced algorithms, the ability to scale, and the capabilities to prepare the data that you want to work with.

There are also a few other things that we need to know when it comes to machine learning to help us really understand how this is going to work and why machine learning is such a great part of technology that we are able to work with as well. Some of the interesting facts that we should know include:

1. When you are working with machine learning, the target is going to be known as a label.
2. When you are looking at the world of statistics, the target is going to be known as a dependent variable.
3. A variable in the world of statistics is going to be known as a feature of machine learning.
4. A transformation in statistics is going to be known as a process of feature creation when you do machine learning

Almost any kind of business that you want to run can utilize machine learning though it is sometimes expensive and time consuming so you really need to take a look at the product you have and the information you want to sort through to determine if this is actually the right option to help you out. For really competitive industries or larger companies with a ton of data, this may be the best data to look through and learn about. As you explore more with machine learning and what it is able to provide to you, you may be amazed at how many different types of companies and industries are going to rely on the ideas and the different algorithms that come with machine learning.

With this in mind, we need to take a look at some of the different methods that are popular when it comes to machine learning. The two most commonly used methods are going to be supervised machine learning and unsupervised machine learning. But there are a few other methods that come with machine learning that you are able to work with as well. Let's explore these a bit to see how they are alike and different, what they can do in machine learning, and why they are so important.

The first type of machine learning algorithm that we are going to explore is supervised machine learning. These ones are going to be trained with the help of examples that have been labeled, such as when the input is given with the desired output known. For example, you could have a piece of equipment that has some data points labeled either F for failed or R for runs. The learning algorithm is going to be able to receive a set of inputs with the outputs that are correct for them. The algorithm is going to be able to step in and learn when it compares the actual output with the correct outputs in order to find the errors that may be present.

From there, it is going to be able to modify the different model that it is using accordingly. Through methods including gradient boosting prediction, regression, and classification, this kind of learning algorithm is going to use some patterns in order to predict the values of the label on an additional data that is unlabeled. Supervised learning is going to be used in many cases where the application is going to use historical data that can predict how likely events in the future are. For example, it is going to anticipate for a financial institution when a credit card transaction is most likely to be fraudulent or when an insurance customer is likely to file a claim.

The next type of learning that we need to take a look at here is going to be the unsupervised learning. This one is going to be the type of learning that is going to be used against a set of data that doesn't have historical labels with it. The system is going to be given the data, but it will not be told the right answer in the process. The algorithm needs to be able to figure out what the information is and what trends are there based on what it sees.

The goal with this one is to get the algorithm to explore the data and then find a structure that is inside. This kind of algorithm can often work well when you do some transactional data. For example, it is able to identify some segments of customers who have attributes in common for marketing campaigns. Or it is going to be able to look at some of the main attributes that are going to help take a large customer base and segment them out into groups that are alike or similar to each other.

There are many different types of techniques that we are able to use with this one, but some of the ones that most programmers are going to work with will include singular value decomposition, k-means clustering, nearest neighbor mapping, and self-organizing maps. These algorithms are also going to be used to segment things like recommended items, text topics, and can help us to see some of the outliers in our information.

The next kind of learning that we are going to focus on are the semi supervised learning. This is going to be a bit different than the other two that we have talked about but can still be valuable to look through and it will use a lot of the same kinds of applications that we have seen with supervised learning.

However, this is going to be slightly different because this kind of learning algorithm is going to be able to rely on both labeled and unlabeled data to help with training. Typically, this means that it is going to use a small amount of data that is labeled and has been mixed in with a large amount of data that is not labeled at all. This is because data that is not labeled is going to be easier to get ahold of and is not as expensive as some of the other options.

There are a few different ways that you are able to work with this kind of learning and some of the options are going to include prediction, regression, and classification. It is also something that you are going to use when you find that the cost associated with labeling is too high for you to allow for training that is fully labeled. Some of the earlier examples of how this kind of machine learning algorithm would be used was when it was used to identify a face of someone on their web cam.

And finally, we can also work with a type of machine learning algorithm that is known as reinforcement learning. This is the kind that is often used with things like navigation, gaming, and robotics. With this kind of learning, the algorithm is going to discover through a process of trial and error which actions are going to provide them with the greatest rewards.

With this kind of learning, there are going to be three components that are going to be important. The first part of this is the agent, or the decision maker and learner. The second part is going to be the environment, which will be everything that the agent is able to interact with. And then the third part is the actions, which are everything that the agent is able to do. The objective in all of this is for the agent to choose the actions that are going to maximize the expected reward as much as possible over a given amount of time. the agent is going to reach the goal much faster when it is able to follow a policy that is good. So, the main goal that comes with the reinforcement learning is to learn the best policy that it needs to follow.

As you can see, each of the different types of machine learning that you are able to work with are going to be different and they are meant to handle a lot of the different parts that come with machine learning and the data analysis that you are going to work with over time. You have to figure out what kind of data you are working with, and the kind of project that you want to solve before you are able to determine which of these algorithms you will need to use.

There is a lot that you are able to do when it comes to working on machine learning. There are already a lot of different types of technologies that are going to rely on machine learning and the different algorithms that come with it. For example, if you have ever worked with a speech recognition device on your phone, or worked with a search engine, then you have worked with machine learning as well.

These are just a few of the examples of what you are able to do when it comes to the technology of machine learning. There are already a lot of examples that are out there about machine learning, and we may not even realize how much this is being used in the world around us. Add in that we are able to work with a lot of new things in the future, and there are a lot of applications and uses for this technology that have not been thought of yet, and our future with artificial intelligence and machine learning is just going to grow.

There is so much potential that can come with working with machine learning, and you are going to find that it can be brought out and used with almost any kind of artificial intelligence and advanced learning process that you want to do with a particular program. Learning how to work with machine learning and all that it entails can make some of this work a bit easier.

Chapter 3: An Introduction to Python

Now that we have had some time to look at the idea of deep learning and artificial intelligence, as well as the ever popular machine learning that is becoming more popular all of the time, it is time to take a look at some of the things that we need to know when we are working with Python. While there are a lot of different options if you want to do artificial intelligence and machine learning, but none of them are going to add the power, the ease of use, and the variety of features and libraries that you can find with Python.

There are a lot of different reasons why you would want to work with Python to help you to get done some of the machine learning algorithms, and some of the deep learning that you would like to accomplish in the process. It may be a programming language that was designed with the beginner in mind, but it has a lot of benefits that come with it, and it is going to be able to handle a lot of the powerful and complex things that you are doing with machine learning as well.

While we are going to take some time to look at the different libraries that are available with Python and how they work to handle some of the other topics that we have talked about before, we need to start out our discussion with some of the basics that come with Python, some of the benefits of choosing this coding language over some of the others that are there, and how this language is going to be able to do with machine learning.

First, let's take a look at what Python is all about. This is an object-oriented programming language that is designed with the beginner in mind. In the past, many of the other coding languages can do a lot of different things that are pretty amazing, but they were often hard to learn and you had to spend a ton of time figuring them out. These would often deter those who wanted to learn because they were just too difficult and there were just too many things that would move around and may no sense to someone who was just starting out.

With Python, things were a bit different. There are a few reasons for this, but one was that the objects were based on things in real life and allowed the user to know where they were and hold them in the same place the whole time. this made life a bit easier overall and avoided a lot of information moving around or getting lost in the process.

In addition to this, the coding language is easy to read, being done in English, and the work that you need to do is gong to be kept to a minimum. There are no extra lines that are not necessary, and even as you read through some of the different options that we talk about in this guidebook, and some of the examples that we provide, you will find that it is easy to read through them, even before you get started and even know what they mean.

As we are talking about this though, you may be a bit nervous about using the language. Maybe it seems a bit strange that you would need to use a language that is designed for beginners to help do things like machine learning and more complicated tasks. But you will find that this language, even though it is maybe easier than some of the other languages out there, and designed with the beginner in mind, is meant to have a lot of power as well. As we go through some of the libraries below that work well with machine learning and artificial intelligence, Python is still the perfect language to help you get all of these algorithms and tasks that you want to do.

This is just the start of some of the benefits that you are going to enjoy when you decide to work with the Python coding language. Another benefit is all of the different libraries that come with this language as well. The basic library of Python is going to be pretty simple to work with and can add in a lot of the functionality that you need with coding. This is great news, but you can take this a bit further and watch how adding some of the extensions and other libraries that are available with Python are going to increase what you can do as well. This can help with things like machine learning, mathematical equations, science, engineering, and more that the traditional library of Python may not be able to handle on its own.

The community support available with Python is something that a lot of programmers enjoy as well. Python is one of the most widely used programs in the world. Because of all the benefits that we have talked about in this chapter, many programmers, beginners and more advanced, throughout the world are using Python to handle all of their programming needs. This provides you with a great community of other individuals who are interested in helping you learn how to work with Python, answering your questions, and so much more.

It is easy to test the code. As you are working on your code, there is going to be some time when you need to be able to test out your code and make sure that it is working the way that you would like. And Python makes it easier to get this done, even as a beginner. Rather than worrying about messing up with the test, or deciding that you don't need to work on the testing at all because you don't know what you are doing, Python testing is easier, giving you the peace of mind to know that things will work when the program is done.

It works well with machine learning. And the number one biggest benefit that comes with working on Python is that it is going to work well with machine learning. There are a lot of different parts of machine learning, and often you can choose to go with another kind of coding language if you would like. But when it comes to power and ease of use, and the different libraries that work specifically well with machine learning like Python does. These are just a few of the reasons why Python is going to work so well with artificial intelligence and machine learning as well.

As you can see here, there are a lot of different benefits that come with working on Python machine learning, and Python can really be a great language that you should spend your time learning about and understanding. It is simple with a lot of power, has all of the extensions and capabilities that you are looking for when working on a programming language, and can help you to handle any of the machine learning algorithms and tasks that you would like to get done. And that is why we are going to spend more time in the rest of this guidebook exploring all of the libraries and methods that you can use to make Python work with machine learning.

Chapter 4: The Scikit-Learn Library

There are also a few different libraries that we are able to use with the help of Python that are going to ensure that we are able to do what we want in the world of machine learning. The regular library that comes with Python is not able to handle all of the functions and the algorithms that need to come with machine learning, but this is where a few of the different library extensions that come with Python can be helpful. The first library that we are going to explore in this guidebook is going to be Scikit-Learn.

We also need to take some time to learn about Scikit-learn. This is going to provide your users with a number of supervised and unsupervised learning algorithms through a consistent Python interface. We are going to take some time to learn more about Python later in this guidebook, but it is a fantastic tool that you are able to use to enhance your machine learning, and since it is for beginners, even those who have never worked with coding in the past will be able to use it.

The Scikit-learn was developed in 2007by David Cournapeau as a Google Summer of code project. This process is going to be suitable to use whether you need it commercially or academically.

Scikit-learn has been in use as a machine learning library inside of Python. It is going to come with numerous types of classification, regression, and clustering to help you get more results. Some of the algorithms that you will get to use with this system is going to include DBSCAN, k-means, random forests, support vector machines, and gradient boosting to name a few. And Scikit-learn was designed so that it would work well with some of the other popular libraries that are found on the Python code, including with SciPy and Numpy libraries.

This particular library was one that was developed to work all in Python, and then there are a few of the algorithms that work here that are more written in Cython instead. This ensures that the programmer who uses all of this is going to get some high-quality performance in the process. You will find that this library has a lot of different features and parts that make it perfect for getting some of that machine learning done, and will ensure that you are going to be able to do many of the different algorithms that you want.

With this in mind, it is now time for us to focus a bit on how to set up the environment that you want to work with. You have to go through a few steps in order to figure out how to get this library installed on your computer and ready to go. Luckily this one is pretty easy to work with so you will have it up and running in no time, with all of the abilities that you want when it comes to writing out the chosen codes.

To start with, remember here that Scikit-Learn is going to work the best on newer versions of Python. It is not supported on any version that is older than Python 2.7 so if you are working on an older version, you are going to need to upgrade in order to use this particular library. Before you decide to install this library though, you also need to double check that there are two other libraries present on your system; the NumPy and the SciPy libraries as well.

These two libraries are going to be the basis of getting the Scikit-Learn library to function properly. They contain some of the functions and variables and other parts that come in the compiler that you will need to focus on as well and can make it easier to actually get some of the work done that you want. Without these in place, it is going to be hard to get the functionality that you need from this Python library.

If you have worked with other parts of machine learning already, then these are probably already on your system and you are ready to go. If this is the first time that you are doing anything with Python or machine learning, then add in these libraries to get things started. If these are not present, then it is time to install them first because they are the basis of Scikit-Learn, and then add this into the mix as well.

The installation of all of these important libraries can be done with the help of pip. This is a type of tool that comes with Python, which means that if you have already installed Python on your system, or once you are done with the installation, then you will get pip. From here, you will be able to use the following command in order to get the scikit-learn ready to go:

pip install scikit-learn

From here the installation will be able to run and then it will complete once all of that is done. It is also possible for you to go through and use the option of conda to help install this library. The command that you will want to use to make sure that this happens is:

conda install scikit-learn

Once you notice that the installation of scikit-learn is complete, it is time to do some importation to get it over to the Python program. This step is necessary in order to use the algorithms that come with it. The good news is that the command to make this happen is going to be done. You simply need to go to your command line and type in import sklearn.

If your command is able to read through what you have written above, and there isn't an error message that shows up, then you know that this installation has been successful overall and you can start using this library as you wish. Take some time to explore around what it has to offer and just familiarize yourself with the environment, and how it is meant to work.

Don't worry too much right now that you don't know how to work with all of the library or that you don't know how all of the coding is supposed to go. This is going to come in a bit. We will spend a few chapters looking at all of the different machine learning algorithms that you are able to do with this Python library, and you will learn that even some of the more complicated tasks can become easy to work on when you use this program overall.

Chapter 5: Creating a Neural Network with Scikit-Learn

Before we start to introduce the TensorFlow library in the next chapter, we are going to take a little detour and learn a bit more about some of the things that you are able to do with the Scikit-Learn library. In particular, we are going to explore the world of neural networks, and how these can be used in order to help us to really do some amazing things with the coding that comes our way.

To start with, the neural networks that you encounter are going to be a great example of what unsupervised machine learning algorithms are going to look like. These types of networks are going to be used because they can find a lot of the different patterns that are present in the data that you go through. This can be done on a ton of different levels and in a way that is actually going to be more effective, and way faster, than what we would see with a person who looked through the data.

When we are looking at how these neural networks are going to work, each of the layers will be searched through by the algorithm to see whether or not there is some kind of pattern in the image. If the network is going through the layer and finds that it can't find a new pattern then it is going to make its prediction. But if it sees a new pattern in that one level, it will remember this information and move on to the next layer to see which patterns are going to be there. Depending on the complexity of the image and how new the neural network system is, it could take some time, and quite a few layers before the system is able to make a prediction. But it is going to get better and better at doing this the more that it practices.

At this point, there is the potential for a few things to happen and it is going to be based on how you set up this program. If the algorithm was able to go through the process that we have listed above, and it was successful at sorting through all of the different layers it would then be able to make a prediction of some sort. If the system is right with the prediction that it makes, then the system is going to remember this information and will become stronger in the future, while making better predictions as time goes on.

The reason that this works is because the neural network is using artificial intelligence, which we talked about earlier, in order to help it learn, and to make sure that there is a strong association, and one that grows, between the objects and the patterns that it is going to see. The more times that the system can come back and provide the user with the right answer, the more efficient the algorithm is going to become.

For those who have not explored all that you are able to do with machine learning and artificial intelligence, it may seem like we are talking about something that is impossible. But when we take a closer look at these neural networks and what all they are able to provide, you will be able to see how they work a bit more, and you will see that the idea of them being able to make decisions and sort through patterns and trends efficiently isn't as far fetched as it may seem.

For example, let's say that you have a goal to make one of your own programs, and you want this program to look over a picture that you add in and figure out what image is there. Through the neural networks, you will be able to go through a few different layers, and maybe many, and some of the information that the algorithm already knows, and then it can tell you that there is a car or a person or something else in the picture.

If you have been able to go through the steps properly and you know the algorithm is set up the right way, then the neural network will be able to make the right predictions that there is already a car in the picture. The program will come up with this kind of prediction based on the features that it knows belong to the car, including the license plate, the color, and more. When you are doing some of the coding that happens traditionally, this is going to be a kind of process that is almost impossible to work with. But with machine learning, and especially with the neural networks, you will find that this system is easier to work with and can be possible in no time.

As the programmer, you do need to do a bit of work. You have to provide the algorithm with a series of information, so it knows what to do, and how to make good predictions. When it is all set up and ready to go, you would then step in and provide the system or the machine that you are using with an image of the car. The neural network is going to take some time, going layer by layer, to look over the picture before making a prediction.

For this process to work, the neural network would start with the very first layer, which could be something like the outside edges of the picture, or of the object that is inside. Then it would continue on with this path going through all of the other layers that are present in that image. When the program is done, it is going to be able to make a prediction about what is inside the image. If the program is able to make a good prediction, it is going to hold onto that information and it will get better at remembering that image again if it encounters another one like it.

There could potentially be a lot of different layers that come with this one, but the more layers and details that the neural network can find, the more accurately it will be able to predict what kind of car is in front of it. If your neural network is accurate in identifying the car model, it is going to learn from this lesson. It will remember some of these patterns and characteristics that showed up in the car model and will store them for use later. The next time that they encounter the same kind of car model, they will be able to make a prediction pretty quickly.

When working with this algorithm, you are often going to choose one, and use it, when you want to go through a large number of pictures and find some of the defining features that are inside of them. For example, there is often a big use for this kind of thing when you are working with face recognition software. All of the information wouldn't be available ahead of time with this method. And you can teach the computer how to recognize the right faces using this method instead. It is also one that is highly effective when you want it to recognize different animals, define the car models, and more.

There are a lot of advantages that come with using this kind of model for machine learning. One of these advantages is that you are going to be able to do this method without having to control the statistics of the algorithm. Even if you don't have the statistics available, or you don't know how to use them, you will find that the neural networks can be used to ensure that any complex relationship that is there is going to show up. This is true between both the variables that are independent and dependent, and even if these variables are nonlinear.

This method is not always going to be the machine learning algorithm that you want to work with, but there are a lot of benefits that come with using it. One of the bigger issues that can show up with this is that the cost of doing the algorithm is going to be high. For some projects, and even for a lot of smaller businesses, this is just going to be too expensive and take up too much computational power to get it done.

Chapter 6: The TensorFlow Library

With that information under our belts and a little bit better understanding of how The Scikit-Learn library is meant to work, it is time to move on to the second library that we are going to focus on in this guidebook. This one is known as the TensorFlow library and it can do some amazing things in the Python language as well. So, let's take some time to explore this library and all that it can offer for us in machine learning.

Another thing that we need to take a look at here is the library that is known as TensorFlow. This is a type of framework that is going to come to us from Google and it is used when you are ready to create some of your deep learning models. This TensorFlow is going to rely on data-flow graphs for numerical computation. And it has been able to stop in and make machine learning easier than ever before.

It makes the process of acquiring the data, training some of the models of machine learning that you want to use, making predictions, and even modifying some of the future results that you see easier. Since all of these are important when it comes to machine learning, it is important to learn how to use TensorFlow.

This is a library that was developed by Google's Brain team to use on machine learning when you are doing it on a large scale. TensorFlow is going to bring together machine learning and deep learning algorithms and models and it makes them much more useful via a common metaphor. TensorFlow is going to use Python, just like what we say before, and it gives its users a front-end API that can be used when you would like to build applications, with the application being executed to a high-performance C++.

Remember here that TensorFlow is able to help out with a lot of the different programming things that you need to do. It is used to help with building, training, and even running some of the neural networks that can be used, especially those that are meant to help with natural language processing, recurrent neural networks that we will talk about in a moment, and for image recognition.

With this in mind, it is time for us to take a look at not only how TensorFlow works, but how we are able to download this onto our system as well. This TensorFlow library is going to be a great one to use for many of the projects that we will discuss in this guidebook, and it comes with the APIs that you need to help with coding in Go, C++, Java, and Rust to name a few. We are going to take a look at all of the steps that you are going to need to follow in order to install this library with a Windows computer.

It is possible to install this kind of library on any kind of operating system that you would like, and it is going to follow a similar kind of process to get it all done. But we are going to focus on getting it done on just one for now, the Windows system, so that we can see some of the basics that we need to get this started. if you want to download this coding library on a Windows computer, you get the choice to install it with the help of either a pip or with the Anaconda extension.

To start with this, the native pip is going to be there in order to help us take the library of TensorFlow and then install it on your chosen system, without having to worry about it being on an environment or not. This may seem like a great option, and in many cases it is, but one thing that we need to remember here is that installing TensorFlow with a pip can sometimes cause other issues because it will interfere with other parts of Python that you have on the system, and that you may be using.

The good news to solve some of this is that the only thing you will need to run to get the pip to work is a single command. And after you have had a chance to get this command to work, TensorFlow is going to be installed and can be used in any manner that you would like on the system. And when this library is installed with the use of that native pip, the user is going to be given the option at this time to run the program from any of the directories that are available on their current system.

You also get the choice of installing the TensorFlow library with the help of the extension of Anaconda. To do this, you first need to make sure that you have created your own virtual environment. However, when you do look through some of the steps that come with Anaconda, you may see that it is going to still recommend that there is some form of a pip install that comes with this, rather than working with the conda install. This is usually because it is easier and can get the work done much faster.

Before we go through some of the coding that you need to use to finish this up, and before we are done with the install, we need to figure double check which version of Python is going to be used with this. It is best if you are able to go with a version of Python that is no lower than Python 3.5. This is the one that is going to have all of the latest features of Python and can be the easiest one to work with overall. And you get the benefit of using the pip 3 install during this process as well.

Another thing to consider is that there are two different versions of this library that you can work with. Their coding is pretty much the same, but it depends on which version that you would like. You can choose to go with either the CPU or the GPU version of this program based on your own preferences. The code that you need to use in order to download the CPU version of TensorFlow to use with Windows includes:

pip3 install – upgrade tensorflow

if you would like to make sure that you are installing the GPU version of the Tensorflow program, you would need to go through and use the following command to make it happen:

pip3 install – upgrade tensorflow-gpu

This is going to ensure that you are able to install TensorFlow on the Windows system that you are using. But another option that you can use to install this library so that you can use it with Python and all of your other machine learning algorithms will include being able to install it with the help of the Anaconda package.

Pip is a program that is automatically going to get installed when you get Python on your system. But the Anaconda program isn't. this means that if you would like to make sure that TensorFlow is able to get installed with the use of the Anaconda program, you first need to take the time to install this program. To do this, visit the website for Anaconda, download it from the website, and then find the instructions for installation from that same site.

Once you are done with this part and the Anaconda program is installed on your system, you should notice that there is a new package that comes with it known as conda. This is a good package that you are going to use on a regular basis, and you should actually stop here for a bit and look through it. It can help you to manage your environment and more all in one place.

You can now go over to the main screen for Windows, click on the button for Start, and then choose on the tab for All Programs here we need to expand out the information and see Anaconda. You can click on the prompt for this so that it launches the Anaconda program on your system. If you wish to look through some of the details that are available on a particular package, you just need to run the command of "conda info". This is a simple code but will give you a chance to read all of the details about the package as well as the manager for that particular package.

There is something else that you may find interesting when it comes to using the Anaconda package, and this is that it is going to help you to not rely on another virtual environment from Python, but will go through the process of helping you to create your own to use. This new environment is going to be like its own little copy of Python that is isolated, with all of the capabilities of maintaining all of the files that it needs, along with all of the paths and all of the directories. This is a great thing because you can do the work that you need in one version of Python, or any of the other libraries that you choose, without having a negative affect on some of the other projects that you may be trying to do in the process.

You will find that having one of your own virtual environments can be a great thing because they can provide the user with a method that helps to isolate projects, and you can then make sure that you avoid any of the potential problems that can show up if you are sharing an environment Note that this is an environment that is going to be different from the normal environment that you will use with Python. This is important to keep in mind because it is going to help you to get the work done, without any negative parts happening in your other projects.

At this point, we are going to work to create a virtual environment for the TensorFlow package.

This can be done with the help of the conda create command. Since we are going to create an environment that is known as tensorenviron, you would use the syntax that is below:

conda create -n tensorenviron

At this point, the program is going to ask you whether or not you would like to allow the process of creating the environment to continue on, or if you would like to cancel the work that you are doing. You will want to type in the "y" and then hit the enter key to move on. This will allow the installation to continue on successfully to see the results that you want.

After you have gone through and created this kind of environment, you will need to take some time to activate it. Without the right activation, you won't be able to use this new environment that you have set up. The activation is going to be done with the help of the activate command. And then you will list out the name of the environment that you want to work with. An example of how you would pull up the environment that you just created includes:

Activate tensorenviron

Now that you have been able to activate the TensorFlow environment, it is time to go ahead and make sure that the package for TensorFlow are going to be installed too. You are able to do this by using the command below:

Conda install tensorflow

When you get to this part of the coding, your computer is going to be able to present you with a longer list of all the different types of packages that you are able to install, and it also comes with the package that is needed for TensorFlow. You will be given a prompt to decide whether you want to download it all at once, or just little parts of it at a time. You can then type in Y and hit enter on your keyboard to get the program to proceed.

Once you have gotten to this point and agreed to all of this, the installation package is going to start doing its work right away. However, notice that the process for doing this installation will take at least a few minutes, if not longer, and the amount of time that it will take to complete is going to depend on how much speed you have on your computer and with your internet provider. This can take at least a few minutes to complete so give it some time.

After the installation process is all done, you can then move on and take a few steps to check whether the installation process was a successful one or not. This is an easy process to do because you just need to go through and run the statement for importing with Python. The statement is going to be done from the Python terminal, and if you are doing this using the prompt that comes with Anaconda, then you just need to type in one word, 'python' and then hit on your enter key. This will make sure that you are going to be in the chosen terminal, and then you can go through the process of using the code below to help continue on:

Import tensorlow as tf

If you find that the package wasn't installed in the proper manner, you are going to end up with an error message on the screen after you do this code. If you don't see an error message, then you know that the installation of the package was successful.

Chapter 7: K-Nearest Neighbors and K-Means Clustering

In this chapter, we are going to spend some time looking at two of the different algorithms that you are able to work with in order to help do a few different processes with Python machine learning. These two that are the focus of our coding will include the K-Nearest Neighbors, or KNN, and the K-Means clustering. These are two popular algorithms that you are able to work with, and knowing how to use them, when they can be beneficial, and more can be critical to helping you to really see some results.

First, we are going to take a look at KNN. This one is going to be used to take some of the data that you present and search through it for the k most similar examples of any kind of instance that you would like to work with. When this is done, then the algorithm is going to look through all of the data, even if you have a lot of data, in order to help you have a summary of it all. Then the algorithm can take the results that it provides to you in order to make predictions for you.

Any time that you decide to work with this particular model, you may find that the learning is going to work well because it becomes really competitive. The reason that this is helpful is because there is going to be some competition that happens between the various parts of the algorithm, or even the different elements, in the various models so that you can end up with the best predictions based on any data that you have.

As you get to working on the KNN algorithm, you will notice that it is a bit different compared to some of the other algorithms that we are going to discuss in this guidebook. For example, in some cases programmers would consider this as a lazier approach to learning because it isn't going to actually go through and create a model for you, at least not until you actively go in and make a new prediction.

Depending on what kind of situation you are trying to work on with that information, this can sometimes be a good thing for your project. This ends up being beneficial because waiting to make new predictions is going to help you to have data that is always up to date, or at least data that you want inside the algorithm. This ensures that you are not going to end up with predictions that are not valid or useful for what you need.

If you had this program work in a different manner, such as having it do predictions at regular intervals, or each time that you inserted some new data, it could be helpful if the situation needed it. But then there are times when you want to just look at a specific customer group or certain information, and this constant updating is not going to be good for what you need The KNN algorithm will make sure that the updates and the new predictions only happen when you want them to.

You will find as you work with this kind of algorithm that there are a number of benefits to using it. When you do bring out the KNN algorithm, you are going to find that it is easier to cut through some of the noise that shows up in the set of data. This noise is sometimes really loud if you are working through a ton of data, and getting rid of some of that noise, especially when it starts to get really distracting, can make it easier to look at the information and the data in front of you and see what trends and patterns are actually there, and what you are able to do with them.

In addition, if your company is trying to deal with and sort through a lot of data at the same time, then the KNN algorithm is going to be the best choice for you. Unlike a few of the other algorithms that are in this guidebook or some of the other ones that you may read about, this algorithm is going to work well because there are no limits on the data size that it is able to sort through.

However, there are going to be a few potential issues that can come up when you are working with this algorithm. To start with the costs of computation are going to be much higher. This is even more true when you try to compare it to some of the other algorithms that could handle similar or the same kind of work. The reason that the costs here are going to turn up higher is because the algorithm will take all of the data, and then sort through every little point that it can, rather than trying to cluster them and send over a prediction.

When the system has to actually look at each individual point, and in large sets of data that could be millions of points, it is going to take a lot of power and time and this is where the extra costs will come in. after this section we will take a look at the K-Means clustering and see why the clustering process can sometimes be a beneficial choice.

With that said, the KNN algorithm can be a great one for you to use in order to see some great benefits with your work and to help you really sort out all of the different data points and information that you have, even when the set of data is really large and seems impossible to go through.

Learning the steps that we will go through below will make sure that you are set up and ready to work with this machine learning algorithm.

How does the K-Nearest algorithm work?

Now that we have taken a few minutes to discuss this kind of algorithm and all that can come with it, it is time to take a look at some of the steps that you need to follow to make sure that you can use the KNN algorithm in the proper manner. Some of the best steps to use to get started with the KNN algorithm are going to include:

1. Load the data into the algorithm for it to read through.
2. Initialize the value that you are going to use and rely on fork.
3. When you are ready to get the predicted class, iteration from one to total number of the data points that you use for training, you can use the following steps to help.
    a. Start by calculating the distance that is in between each of your test data,

and each row of your training data. We are going to work with the Euclidean distance as our metric for distance since it's the most popular method. Some of the other metrics that you may choose to work with here include the cosine and Chebyshev.

b. Sort the calculated distances going in ascending order, based on their distance values.

c. Get the k rows from the sorted array.

d. Get the most frequent class for these rows.

e. Return back the class prediction.

The K-means clustering

The next algorithm that we are going to spend some time looking at is known as the k-means clustering. This is a basic idea that is found with a lot of different kinds of algorithms in this topic, but this is one of the easiest, and most common, forms of clustering that you are able to work with.

It is also a good example of unsupervised machine learning as well. It is going to be applied in most cases when the data that you have doesn't come with labels that are on it. The goal of working with this algorithm to ensure that you can see the clusters or the groups that are found inside your data.

The whole point of these clusters is that the objects that are found in the same cluster are going to be closely related to the other points that fall into that same cluster. In addition, these points are not going to have as many similarities to the items that are found in any other cluster that you set up. The similarity here is going to be a metric used to see how strong the relationship between the objects are in the set of data.

There are a variety of times when you would use this kind of clustering, but one example is when you are doing the process of data mining, especially if the data mining is more exploratory. It could also have uses in other kinds of fields, including some that have to go with compressing data, image analysis, computer graphics, pattern recognition, and machine learning to list out a few.

When you use this kind of algorithm, it is going to help you to form up some of the data clusters that you need, based on the values that come with your data. As a programmer, it is then your job to go through and specify out what you want the value of k to end up being. This means that you need to determine how many clusters you would like the algorithm to make out of the data. The algorithm is then going to take the value of K and use it to select the centroid value for all of the clusters that you are working with.

When the steps above are done, it is then time for the k-means algorithm to go through and complete three more steps. These steps are going to include:

1. You will want to start with the Euclidian distance between each data instance and the centroids for all of the clusters.
2. Assign the instances of data to the cluster of centroid with the nearest distance possible.

3. Calculate the new centroid values, depending on what the mean values of the coordinates of the data instances from the corresponding cluster.

Writing out the formula for K-means clustering

So the first step that we will need to do is to calculate the cluster responsibilities. The formula we will use is the following:

r(kn) = exp[-b * d(m(k), x(n))] / sum[j=1..K] { exp[-b * d(m(j), x(n))] }

From here, you can see that the r(k,n) is going to work out as a fraction, some number that is in between 0 and 1, where you can interpret the hard k-means or the regular k-means to be the case where r(k,n) is always exactly equal to 0 or 1. The d(*,*) can be any valid distance metric, but the Euclidean or squared Euclidean distances are the ones that are used the most.

Then for the second step, we are going to work on a formula that is similar to the hard k-means, but we are just recalculating the means based on the responsibilities that we want to send with it. The algorithm that we are going to use for this includes:

$$m(k) = sum[n=1..N] \{ r(k,n)* x(n)] / sum[n-1..N] \{ r(k,n) \}$$

so, when you take the time to look at this algorithm above, you are going to see that it is similar to the weighted mean. This is going to show you that if the r(k,n) is higher, then the mean is going to be more important to the cluster of k. When you see this, it is going to show that this is going to have the biggest influence on the calculation of the mean. But if the mean is higher when you look at the algorithm, you will know that the opposite is true.

Clustering algorithms can be really useful when it comes to working with machine learning and some of the other choices that come with computer sciences, and the k-means clustering is a great way to gain some experience with doing all of this and ensuring that you are going to get everything matched up and working the way that you would like. Make sure to learn some of the equations above, and some of the benefits of these carious algorithms, so that you can use them for your computing needs when necessary.

Chapter 8: Decision Trees and Random Forests in Machine Learning

The next kind of machine learning algorithm that we are going to look at are going to include the decision tree and the random forest. These work together because a bunch of decision trees can make up a random forest. These are great tools to use when you need to see which decision is the best for your company, and you want to compare and contrast the different decisions that you are able to make. let's first explore a bit more what these decision trees are all about, and then we can dive into some more about how they work together to make up a random forest.

To start with the decision tree is going to be a good tool for data and can be efficient if you would like to take a look at more than one choice, and you know the choices are going to be completely different. You can gather up information on both choices and put them into the decision tree to help make the right decision to improve and even to grow your business. When the different options are presented through the decision tree to you, you can use this to see what the potential outcomes of each decision will be in the future. This makes it much easier to make accurate and smart decisions and can help with predictions in the future as well.

As a programmer or even a business owner who wants to use this kind of algorithm, there are a few options when it comes to how you would work with these decision trees. Many of those who are using it are going to use it to help with random or categorical variables. In many cases though, machine learning is going to want you to make these trees as a classification problem.

To help you double check that any decision tree you are making ends up being a good one, you will need to be able to take up all of the sets of data that you want to work with, and then you need to be able to split them up between two, and often more, sets with similar data being found in each of the sets. These can then be sorted out with the help of the independent variables that you can choose from, simply because this ensures that each set is distinguished and set out from all the others.

So, now that we have gotten to this part, it brings up the idea that this can be something that is hard to work on. In order to make sure that the decision tree is going to work the way that you would like, or to at least see how it is going to behave when you try to use it, let's look at a good example of this. In this one, we are going to have a group with 60 people inside of it.

With these people, all of them are going to have three independent variables. These variables are going to include the height of the person, their gender, and what class they are in. Then, when it is time to look at the students who are in that group, you will be able to find out that half of them like to play soccer as well. Using the independent variables that you were presented above, your goal is to figure out which half of the students like to play soccer, and which ones do not like to play this sport.

Going from the information that you have about which kinds of students are the most likely to enjoy playing soccer, you decide that it is time to create a model to help you look at that group of 60 people and decide which 30 out of them like the game of soccer, and which 30 are going to spend their time playing or doing something else.

To make this one work the model needs to be able to go through all of the students who are in the group, or all of the people in your group, and then divide them up into two groups. You need to have a group that is going to be the ones that are going to love playing soccer, and the ones that don't. and you want to make sure that the model is as accurate as possible.

There are some other possibilities that you can work with that work well with the decision tree. These algorithms are useful because it is going to help you to split up all of the data that you have, providing a few different subsets that are going to give you good outcomes that are the most homogenous, and will ensure that all of the decisions that you make based on this information is as accurate as possible. Remember here that you can have more if the situation needs it, but for the example that we are doing here, you will only want to work with two subgroups and no more.

You may find that there are a lot of times when a business or another company will need to go through some data that is complex, and they want to use this information to make decisions and figure out what actions they should take. A decision tree is going to help them to get this done and to provide them with the data they need in an efficient and helpful manner

In the past before working with some of the various machine learning algorithms, like decision trees, a business owner would need to work with their own intuition in order to make their decisions. But the world is much more complex now, and there is a ton of extra information that is out there that is hard to sort through on your own. Relying on some of these algorithms and systems to help you to make your decisions, rather than just guessing and risking a lot of time and money can make a big difference.

Moving to the random forest

Now that we have had some time to explore what the decision tree is all about, it is time to move on to another step of looking at the random forest. There are times when just one single decision tree is going to be enough to help you make some decisions for your needs. But sometimes, you need to compare a lot of different options and you are going to need to work with a group of decision trees, which will make up your own random forest.

These random forests are going to be a popular option to work with when we talk about machine learning. So, if you plan to work with decision trees on machine learning quite a bit, then it is also important to learn how to work with the random forests as well.

Since the random forest algorithm is so popular with a lot of programmer, it is not going to be hard for you to see that it could potentially help you with a lot of different types of problems. For example, if you are looking to work with some tasks that can look through and explore the data that you have, and deal with values that are missing, or you would like to deal with some of the outliers that show up in the data that is there.

There are a lot of times when you are going to be able to use the random forest to help with various parts of machine learning. The random forest is going to be the best way to provide you with results out of complex or large amounts of data. And often this algorithm is going to be able to do a much better job than what you may see with some of the other algorithms that we will talk about in this guidebook. With this in mind, some of the advantages that you can get for working with random forests include:

- When you are working on your own training sets, you will find that all of the objects that are inside a set will be generated randomly, and it can be replaced if your random tree things that this is necessary and better for your needs.

- If there are M input variable amounts, then m<M is going to be specified from the beginning, and it will be held as a constant. The reason that this is so important because it means that each tree that you have is randomly picked from their own variable using M.
- The goal of each of your random trees will be to find the split that is the best for the variable m.
- As the tree grows, all of these trees are going to keep getting as big as they possibly can. Remember that these random trees are not going to prune themselves.
- The forest that is created from a random tree can be great because it is much better at predicting certain outcomes. It is able to do this for you because it will take all prediction from each of the trees that you create and then will be able to select the

average for regression or the consensus that you get during classification.

Before you decide that the random forests are going to be the right tool for you, it is important to remember that they do have some negatives. For example, they are able to help you handle some of the regression problems that come your way, but they will not be able to make predictions past whatever kind of training data you decide to add into it, or the ranges that you are working with when you submit the information.

What this means is that the random forests are going to help you to make some predictions, and they will be the best part of helping you to make some decisions that work well for your business. While there are a lot of benefits that come with it, there are also going to be some limitations because of how far in the future it is able to make the predictions. This lowers the amount of accuracy that you have. Depending on what you are trying to learn about though, you may find that this algorithm is still one of the best for your needs.

Chapter 9: The Linear Classifier and What This Means

As you are going through some of the different parts that come with supervised machine learning algorithms, you may find that two of the most common tasks that you will need to focus on will include either the linear classifier or the linear regression to get things done. The linear regression is useful because it helps you to predict what values you will get, while the linear classifier is that it is going to focus on the class specifically. We are going to take a look at the linear classifier in particular in this chapter, and how you can use it with some of your machine learning.

You will find that when you are trying to use the libraries we talked about earlier in this guidebook to do some machine learning work, that the classification problems are going to take up the majority of your work, often 80 percent of the machine learning tasks that you need to do. The classification is going to aim at predicting how probable it is going to be for each class to occur given the set of inputs that you would need to add in. The label, which is going to be known as our variable that is dependent in this case, is going to be the class, or the discrete value.

If the dependent variable, or our label, is going to work with just two classes in the process, then you know that the learning algorithm you choose is going to be a binary classifier in the end. But if you are working on a classifier that is more multiclass, this means that it is going to be able to tackle the labels that have two classes or more.

Let's look at an example of this. Many times, the classification problems that we are working on that turn out to be binary will be able to help you predict the likelihood that your customer is going to come back to the business again and make another purchase. But if you want to work with a system that is going to make some predictions about the type of animal that shows up in a given picture, then you are working with what is known as a multiclass classification problem because there will be more than two varieties of animals that the program has to deal with.

With this in mind, it is time to measure out the performance of linear classifier that you can work with. Accuracy is one of the best topics to start with here. The performance overall of this classifier is going to be measured by how accurate it can be. Accuracy is able to collect all of the values that are correct that you have, and then it will be able to divide that number by the total number of observations that are present.

Let's say that you have a value of accuracy in the algorithm or the data that you are working with that is about 85 percent. What this is going to mean for you is that when you put that model to use, it is going to provide you with an answer that is right about 85 percent of the time. it will also be incorrect 15 percent of the time. The goal with this one, of course, is to keep the percentage of being correct as high as possible.

At this point, you can already see that there may be a bit of a shortcoming that comes with it when you work on that metric, especially if you are doing a class that includes some imbalance. A set of data that is not balanced very well is going to happen when the amount of observations that show up is not going to be equal in all of the groups that you are working with.

To take this further, let's say that you are working on a classification problem of a rare event with your function of logistics. You can imagine here that the classifier that you are using is going to try and estimate how many patients died when they contracted one kind of disease. In the data that you have, about five percent of the patients who contract this disease are going to pass away from that kind of disease.

With this information in mind, you can then go through and train the classifier to make sure that it can make a god prediction about the number of deaths that end up happening, and then you can work with the accuracy metric in order to evaluate the performance of that hospital or that clinic. Now, if the classifier is able to work and predicts that there are 0 deaths for the whole set of the data, then it is going to show that this model is right about 95 percent of the time when used.

From here, we need to move on and take a look at what is going to be called the confusion matrix. This is one of the better ways available for us to look at the performance of the classifier compared to the accuracy. When you are working with one of these confusion matrix, you will get the benefit of visualizing how the accuracy metric of the classifier is going to be when it is compared to the predicted, and the actual classes that you choose. The binary confusion matrix is going to have a series of four squares and the parts that you are able to see in this kind of matrix is going to include:

1. TP: This is going to known as the true positive. This is going to contain all of the predicted values that were correctly predicted as an actual positive.

2. FP: This is going to be the false ones, or the ones that were predicted in an incorrect manner. They were usually predicted as positive, but they were actually negative. This means that the negative values show up, but they had been predicted ahead of time as positive.
3. FN: This is false negative. This is when your positive values were predicted as negative.
4. TN: this is going to be the true negative. These are the values that were predicted in a correct manner and were predicted as actual negative.

When you take a look at one of these of these confusion matrixes, you will be able to see a clear look at the actual class and the predicted class and see what is going on there.

The next thing that we want to focus on here is how to look at the precision and how sensitive this algorithm can be. You will see that when you create one of your own confusion matrix, there is a lot of information that is going to show up. It is also going to be useful to help us to see some good insights into any of the true and the false positives that will show up here. But there are also some case where it is preferable to have a metric that is a bit more concise than what we have been talking about so far.

To help us out with this, we first need to take some time to look at the precision that comes with the code. This precision metric is going to give us the amount of accuracy that shows up in the positive class. This just means that it comes into play to give us an idea, as well as the measure, or how likely that the prediction of the positive class is actually correct. To help you check this in your own matrix, you will need to use the following code:

Precision = TP/(TP + FP)

The maximum score that you can get here is one. And this is going to show up the classifier perfectly comes up correctly with the positive values. Precision alone is not going to be that helpful because it is going to ignore the negative class. This matric is something that you may want to pair up with the recall metric. The recall is also called sensitivity or true positive rate.

The next thing that we need to take a look at is the sensitivity. This sensitivity is important because it is going to help us compute the ratio of positive classes that the algorithm was able to detect correctly. This metric can be a good way to model and take a look at a positive class. The formula for figuring out the sensitivity is:

Recall = TP/(TP + FN)

How to use the linear classifiers in TensorFlow

Remember earlier how we talked about TensorFlow and all that can come with it. But now it is time to take this a bit further and look at how you are actually able to work with TensorFlow, and how you can really do some great things with machine learning through this Python library.

Now it is time for us to take a look at some of the practical work that we are able to do with the linear classifiers through the TensorFlow library. We are going to take an example of how to work with this using the census data. The purpose of us going through these steps is to make sure that you use a variable in the census data set in order to make sure that we can take a look at the participants we have and can make predictions on how much income they make. note that the income is going to become our variable that is binary for this example.

For this one to work, we are going to set the binary variable to be at one when the individual has an income that is higher than $50,000 a year. But if you have a participant with an income per year that is less than the $50,000, then they are going to have the variable show up as 0. The set of data that we will work with here can be separated out into variables that are categorical, and there are eight of them. These will include the following:

Native country

Sex

Race

Relationship

Occupation

Marital status

Education

And place of work

And on top of this, we are going to take a look in this at six of the continuous variables. These are going to include:

Hours_week

Capital_loss

Capital_gain

Education_num

Fnlwgt

Age

With this information, we can bring up the TensorFlow extension to help us to figure out the probability to see which of our customers, or any individuals in the set of data, are going to fit into the two groups that we set up. These people are going to be separated out into the two groups that we set up before (although you can add in as many groups as you would like based on what kind of program you are doing). IN this one, the two groups will be based on whether the individuals make above or under the $50,000 a year.

When this is done, you will be able to look into the groups that were formed and find out some of the background information that is there, including what gender, their race, where they live, what their occupation is, and so much more. This is a kind of tool that a lot of businesses are turning to and starting to rely on more than ever because it helps them to learn about new and potential customers, as well as repeat customers, and can make their marketing more efficient overall.

What are the differences between discriminative and generative models?

As we are working on some of the parameters that are found with our linear classifier, there are going to show up two separate classes or methods that we need to work with, which are going to be broad at this time, and are meant to help you figure out how to determine where the parameters should be set. The options that you have here are going to be the generative or the discriminative model.

Methods that fit in with the generative model are going to be considered conditional density functions. The two biggest examples that you are going to see of this kind of algorithm is going to be something like the linear discriminant analysis. This is going to be like the Naïve Bayes Classifier or the Gaussian conditional density models.

Then a programmer also gets the choice of working with what is known as the discriminative model. These are important because they are set up to work so that your output will come out as high quality as possible when you do a new set of training. Additional terms in the training can be necessary, but these will cost more overall and could perform what is known as regularization of your final model. The good news is that this model is going to provide you with a few options to make it easier to work with, and these options are going to include the following:

1. Logistic regression. This is going to be the likelihood estimation of linear classifiers assuming that the observed training set was generated by a binomial model that depends on the output of the classifier.
2. Perceptron: This is a type of algorithm that you are going to use because it will try to go through and fix up any and all of the errors that can occur in a training set.
3. Support vector machine: This is one of the options that we talked about before. It is going to be the algorithm that will be able to maximize, as much as possible, the margin that can come between the examples that re in the training set and the decision hyperplane.

Despite the look of the name there, the LDA is not going to belong to the discriminative models in this method. However, the nae does make sense when you are able to compare it to some of the other algorithms that are there, such as with principal components analysis. You will find that the LDA algorithm is going to fit in with supervised learning and it is going to be able to utilize the labels on your data, but the PCA is going to be an algorithm of unsupervised learning, and it purposely goes through and ignores the labels that are present.

As you work with discriminative training, it is easy to find that it can provide you with more of the accuracy that we were talking about before compared to working with the conditional density function. If you are looking to get a higher amount of accuracy out of the work that you are doing, then this is the best algorithm to work with.

However, there are some issues that can come up with it as well. While the discriminative training is going to provide you with some more accuracy along the way, the conditional density models are able to handle some of the missing data points in an easier manner. If your data is missing in a lot of places, or you are concerned about how that missing data is going to affect your predictions, then going with the conditional density models is the best option.

Working with linear classifiers can be a great way to work with some more of the things that we have already talked about with machine learning, while also giving you some more time to learn about and actually use the TensorFlow library as we talked about before. Take some time to work through the equations that we provided above and see just how these linear classification problems can be handled.

Chapter 10: Are Recurrent Neural Networks Different from Neural Networks

We spent some time talking about the neural networks before and how they can work to make predictions and can get stronger the more times they are exposed to inputs and can learn from them. Now we are going to take that a bit further and discuss another topic that is along the same lines, the idea of recurrent neural networks.

When we are doing a study of the human brain, it is reasonable to know that when we think, this process isn't going to restart from nothing every few seconds. We are going to keep building on what we were able to learn in the past. We remember what we learned as a child, or even yesterday when we went through a new process. And we can retain that information for a long time to come. We don't have to relearn how to brush our teeth each day, we just remember how to do that so we can focus on learning new things in the future. This is important because it is going to tell us that the thoughts, we have are going to have persistence and consistency that goes along with them.

With those traditional neural networks from before, you won't see this same kind of process occurring, and sometimes this is going to be a shortcoming that we need to work for. For example, if you would like to be able to go through and classify a kind of event that is happening at different points in the movie, this would be something that the regular neural network that we talked about before would struggle with a bit.

The good thing to remember here is that there is a machine learning algorithm that is able to handle this, and that is the recurrent neural networks. These networks are going to have what are known as loops in them, which makes it easy for the information that it learns to persist, much like it does in the human brain. In this method, the loop is going to be take all of the information that you have and will pass it from one part of your network over to the next. This is going to be similar to what would happen if you had more than one copy of the same network, with each message getting moved on over to the successor has time went on.

This chain like nature is important because it is going to show us how the recurrent neural networks are going to be related pretty closely to the sequences and the lists. They are the natural architecture of the neural network to use for the data. And they will be used on a frequent basis when it comes to machine learning. In the last few years, there has been a lot of people working with these and trying to see how much success they were able to garner from using these kinds of networks.

One of the limitations that come with the recurrent neural networks that is pretty glaring is that the API is going to come with a variety of constraints you have to work through. They are only going to be able to take an input of a fixed sized vector, and they are only able to produce an output that is in a fixed sized vector as well. These models are going to also perform the mapping that you want, but they can only do it within a fixed number of computational steps, which is going to equal the number of layers that you are going to see in the model.

The main reason that these recurrent neural networks are going to be useful and can actually be exciting to use in your coding is that they will allow you as the programmer to operate your own work over a sequence of vectors, rather than just one. This is going to include having these sequences in the input, the output, but oftentimes you will find them in both of these places.

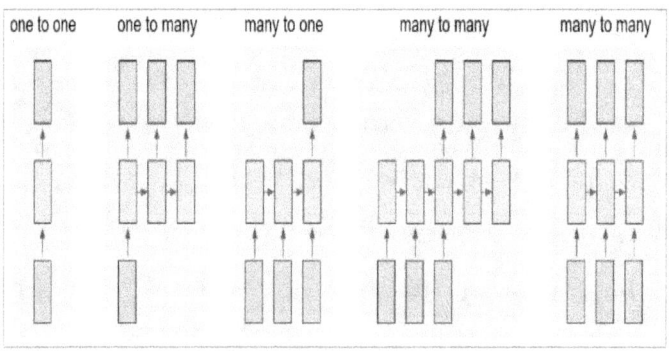

To help us see how these recurrent neural networks are going to work, we need to take a look at the charts above to give us an example. Each of those rectangles above are going to be one of our vectors, and then the arrows are going to be the parts that tell us the functions. The input with the vectors are going to be the ones that are red, and ten the output vectors that we need to know are the ones that show up in blue. You can also see that there are some green vectors present as well ans these are going to hold onto what is known as the state of the RNN. Going from the left diagram over to the right with what is above, let's see how each one is going to work and gain a better understanding of these recurrent neural networks.

1. The first one is going to be the vanilla mode of processing, the one that doesn't use the RNN at all. This is going to include an input that is fixed, and an output that is fixed. This is also known as image classification.
2. Sequence output is going to be the second part. This is going to be image captioning that is able to take an image and then will

provide you with an output of a sentence of words.

3. Sequence input: This is goi going to be the third picture above. It is going to be more of a sentiment analysis that shows us a given sentence and makes sure that it is classified as either a negative or positive sentiment.
4. Sequence output and sequence output. You can find this one in the fourth box, and it is getting a bit closer to what we want. This one is going to be similar to a machine translation. This is when the RNN is able to read a sentence out in English, and then can take that information and provide you with an output that reads the sentence in rench.
5. And finally, the last box is going to be the synced sequence input and output. The video classification here is going to help us to label out each of the frames that occur in a video if we decide to.

Notice that in each of these, there aren't going to be any constraints put on the lengths of the sequences that we have to specify ahead of time.

this is because the recurrent transformation, which is going to be shown in green, is fixed, and we are able to apply it out as many times as we would like, or as many times as work with our project.

Looking at how the RNN algorithm is going to work.

We will now take some time to look at an example of how this kind of algorithm is really going to be able to work for us. In this particular example, we will work to train this algorithm at the mode for the character level language. What this is going to mean is that we are going to provide the RN with a lot of text, and then we are going to ask it to give us a model about the probability of distribution for the next character that should show up in that sequence.

The answer is going to be based on the previous characters that we see. This is a good project to work on because it shows us how the RNN algorithm is going to be able to generate a new text for us, even though it is finding the text with one character at a time.

So, with our program, we are going to assume that we had a really limited and we only had four possible letters to work with. With just this limited amount of information, we want to be able to train our RNN to do a sequence so that it can list out the word of "hello" for us. This training sequence is going to need to include four training examples to see the results. This can sound complex when we first start but we can go through this one step at a time to hep us get a better idea of how this works and to get the letters to show up at the right time and in the right order. Some of the things that we can do to get this to happen will include:

1. The probability of getting "e" should be just as likely to occur as getting the letter "h".
2. "L should be likely in the context of "he"
3. The "l" should also be likely if the system is given the context of "hel"

4. "o" should be likely if the other sequences have happened and the context of "hell" is in place.

With this idea, we are going to take a moment to encode all of the characters that can show up in the vector working with the 1 of k encoding. We will then be able to feed this into the algorithm for RNN that we are working with, one at a time using the right function to get this to happen.

After we have been able to get all of the different parts in place, we are going to be able to observe a sequence of four dimensional output vectors, with one dimension that will show up for each of the characters, which we can then interpret at the confidence that the RNN is able to assign right now to each of the characters that come up in the next sequence at the time. One thing that is going to help us to understand how this can work is with the chart below.

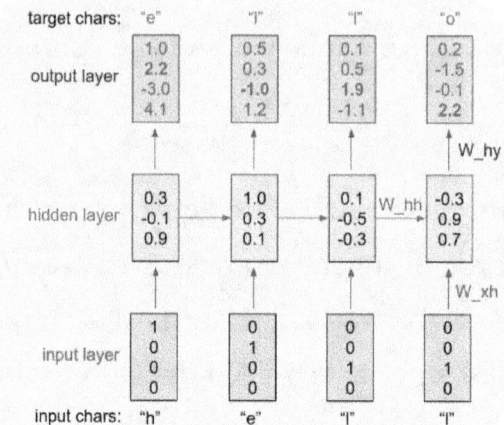

Out of this, we may use an example of seeing that in the first time step, the RNN would see the character of "h" it was able to assign some confidence to this of 1.0, to the next letter turning into "h", 2.2 to getting the letter "e" -3.0 to "l" "and 4.1 to "o". Sine the training data that we are using, (which is the string of hello that we talked about above), had the next right character being "e" we want to increase the confidence, or the green color, and then decrease how confident it is in all of the other letters, which are going to be shown in the red above.

266

In addition to these steps, we are going to be able to take another step here and then come up with the target character that we need here at ever one of our four time steps that we want the network to assign with a good deal of confidence. This is going to take a bit more time to accomplish but it can be helpful because it will help you to make sure that your confidence in the algorithm is as high as possible to ensure you get the right letters in the word to show up at the right time.

Sine we are working with this kind of algorithm, and it is going to be set up to include differentiable operations, we are going to be able to use what is known as the back-propagation algorithm. This algorithm is going to include a recursive application of the chain rule that you may have learned in calculus. We will also be able to use this rule to help us figure out what direction we want to use to adjust the various weights at play. This ensures that we are able to increase the scores of the correct targets which in this example will be the bold and the green numbers

After you have had a chance to do this, it is time to work on the parameter update. This parameter update is going to help us to just nudge over all of the weights a bit, in whichever direction works the best for you. If we are able to double check that the inputs we feed into this algorithm are the same after each of the updates that come with the parameter, we are going to find that the scores of our correct characters would be higher, in this case being between 2.2 and 24, and then the incorrect characters that we do not want to show up will go down for us.

Since we are working on a whole word here, it is likely that we will need to repeat this process more than one time, and often main times, in order to get it to work. How many times you need to do this will often depend on the amount of complexity that comes with the system. We are keeping this pretty easy with just one word, but if you were trying to do a whole paragraph, a whole page, or even a longer document, the number of times you have to go through this would be more difficult.

Since machine learning is going to be a programming technique that has to learn over time, you may need to go through the loop and help it to learn here. Make sure that you are repeating the process until you are able to get this RNN to converge and the predictions end up being consistent with the training data. When this happens, the right characters are going to be predicted in the same and correct order, every time that you decide to run this program.

We can also work with an explanation that is a bit more technical here. And we are able to do this once we work with the standard Softmax classifier, which is sometimes referred to as the cross-entropy loss) on every output vector at the same time. you will be able to train the RNN with the mini-batch Stochastic Gradient Descent, and you may find that working with Adam or RMSProp to make sure that the updates are as stable as possible.

When you do all of this, you should notice that the first time that the character of "l" is inputted to this, the target is "l" but the second time the target is going to be "o". The RNN is not going to be able to just rely on the input on its own, and it is going to need to bring in some recurrent connection to help keep track of the context that is needed to make this task achievable.

When you get to testing time, you will be able to go in and feed the right characters into the RNN algorithm. And once that is put in, you should be able to see the distribution over what characters the system is going to bring out next and see if you get the answers that you want. We will then be able to sample from the distribution that we are given, and then we feed it all right back in to see which letter you are going to get next. You can then just repeat this process until you get everything in the right order, and you will find that you are sampling the text.

As this chapter took some time to point out, the RNN algorithm can be useful and can help you out with a lot of different projects and even problems in machine learning that you just wouldn't be able to do with some of the other algorithms we have discussed before. It will open up more doors and different opportunities to make sure that you can handle more of the situations that you want in machine learning in the process.

Chapter 11: What Else Can I Do with Python Programming and Machine Learning?

We have spent some time in this guidebook talking not only about the Python program, but also about machine learning, artificial intelligence, and deep learning. And the majority of what we have discussed is the different algorithms that you are able to use in order to actually complete some of your own programs in machine learning, of course with the help of the Python programming language.

There are a lot of different machine learning algorithms that you are able to use, and they often work with the various libraries that we have already been able to discuss in this guidebook. Learning how to work on these and why they are important, and when to bring them out for your project, can make machine learning that much easier overall.

With this in mind, there are a ton of other algorithms that work with both Python and machine learning that you are able to focus on, and this chapter is going to discuss a few of them. While we are not going to have time to dive into each and every algorithm that is available for machine learning (and there are always more being developed over time as machine learning grows and becomes even more popular), we are going to take some time to look at a few more of the Python machine learning algorithms that you should know.

Naïve Bayes

The first of these additional machine learning algorithms that we are going to focus on is known as the Naïve Bayes. To help us get a better understanding of the steps that are needed to make this one work properly, we may need to use our imaginations and think about a scenario. Imagine that you are currently working on a project that is meant to be a classification problem, but your goal here is to make sure that you are creating a hypothesis that is new and will actually work with the algorithm that you want. You also want to make sure that any design that you are handling will allow you to have a new discussion or a new feature based on how important each of your variables turns out to be.

While in the beginning this is going to seem like it is a lot of work, and like we are trying to stuff it in all at once, it is something that you are able to do with machine learning. Once you can take some time in order to collect all of the different information that you need, it is likely that a few people within the company are going to be interested at the model you use, and what you plan to do with it. It is possible that these individuals are going to want to see the model and what you are doing long before you are actually ready to present it to them.

As you can imagine here, there is a dilemma. How are you meant to show to the other people in the company what you are doing, and how the model will work, in a manner that they will be able to understand, can be a challenge. And you may not have gotten very far in the work that you are doing yet, so how are you supposed to showcase all of the information yet?

Depending on the kind of problem that you are focusing on it is possible that you would have millions of different points of data to work with, and in the early stages of this model, it is easier to understand how you can be overwhelmed, but there are still steps that you can take in order to make everyone happy and showcase what you are going to do with a model, even to people who may not be able to understand all of the technical stuff, but still need to know what is going on with the information. But how is this all possible?

This is going to work with the Naïve Bayes algorithm, an algorithm that you are able to work with that ensures the programmer is able to stick with some of the earlier stages of the model, one that is easy to understand while you still show any and all of the information that you need at the time.

Let's take a look at how this is going to work with an example of apples. When you grab what is considered an average apple, you will easily be able to state that there are some distinguishing features that are present. This could include the fact that the apple is red, that it is round, and that it will be around three inches round. While these can sometimes be found in some other types of fruits, when all of these features are present together, then we know that the fruit in our hands is an apple. This is a basic way of thinking, but this is an example of working with the Naïve Bayes.

The Naïve Bayes model is meant to be easy for you to put together, and it is sometimes used to help you get through really large sets of data in a way that is simplified. One of the advantages of working with this model is that though it is simple, it is sometimes better to work with compared to the other, more sophisticated models that you can work with.

As you learn more about how to work with this algorithm, you will start to find that there are more and more reasons for you to work with it. This model is really easy to use, especially if you are a beginner to the world of deep learning and machine learning. You will also find that it can be really effective when it is time to make some predictions for our data sets and what class they should end up in. This makes it easier for you to keep things as simple as possible during the whole process. Even though the Naïve Bayes algorithm is really simple to work with, you will find that it is able to perform really well. In fact, when compared to some of the higher-class algorithms that are out there, and some of the ones that seem to be more sophisticated, this one is going to perform the best.

While we have spent some time talking about the different benefits that come with the Naïve Bayes algorithm, there are going to be some negatives that we need to watch out for as well. The first of these negatives is that when you work with this algorithm, one that is going to take on variables that are categorical, you have to make sure that any of the data you test hasn't already gone through a set of data to be trained. This algorithm is also going to struggle with some of the predictions it makes and how much accuracy is found there. The Naïve Bayes is going to rely mostly on probability rather than accuracy so keep this in mind as you go through and work on that data.

There are a few steps that you can take in order to help fight off this issue and to ensure that things are going to work out the way that you would like, it is sometimes confusing to know how to handle these steps and many beginners do not like to do this.

Of course, even with some of these negatives, the Naïve Bayes is going to be a good option to help out when you are doing some work with machine learning. But it is not going to have everything that you need each time that you start programming. For those coders who want to be able to take their information and get it set up in a simplified manner that is easy to read through and won't require you to add in a lot of complicated code, at least not yet, then the Naïve Bayes model is the right one for you.

Working with the regression algorithm

The second Python machine learning algorithm that we are going to focus on here is called the regression analysis. This algorithm is going to help you out when you would like to see whether there is any relationship, and what type of relationship, will show up between the two variables in your code, the predictor variable ad the dependent variable.

This is a technique that often works well when you would like to make sure you can check out whether there is a casual relationship that shows up in the forecasting part of the variable, or the time-series modeling in place. The reason that a programmer would want to work with the regression algorithm at all is that it is able to take ahold of the information that you have, and then can fit it back onto a simple curve, and often a line, as much as possible. There may be some points that are way far away from this line, but the line or the curve is set up to handle the majority of the data points as much as possible.

You will find that the regression algorithm is used by a variety of companies right now because it is so helpful for adding in any information that is needed and then sorting through it and seeing what is there. you can add in information about the current economy, or even the past economy for example, and then this algorithm is going to come up with an output as a prediction of how things will show up in the future. You have to make sure that the information you provide to the algorithm is up to date and accurate though, or this prediction is not going to be that accurate at all.

The thing that a lot of programmers are going to like about using the regression algorithm is that you can add in any kind of information that you need to it. You can add in information to help you know about some predictions on your profits to help you see any estimations it can come up with about the sales growth that may happen in your company. And it can even be used if the right information is added in to tell us more about the economy and how the market is doing now, and how it is likely to do in the future.

Let's take a look at how this can be done first. In this example, if you choose to work with the regression algorithm, and then you find out that the company is growing at a similar rate as what other industries are doing, or even other companies in the same industry, than you would be able to take this information and use it to make some good predictions on how you are likely to do in the future based on what decisions you are planning to make

As you look through the idea of regression algorithms, you will notice that there are more than one kind of regression algorithm that you are able to focus on based on what your end goal is all about and what information you would like the algorithm to show to you when it is all said and done. Some of the different types of regression algorithms that are available for you to try out as you do machine learning will include:

- Linear regression
- Polynomial regression
- Logistic regression
- Ridge regression
- Stepwise regression

As you can see, working with the regression algorithms are going to have a few different benefits that come with them. To start, you will see that these algorithms make it easy for anyone using the information to see what relationship is present, if any, between the dependent variables and the independent variables. This algorithm is also able to show what kind of impact will happen if you try to add in a new variable or change up another kind of variable that is in your data set.

Even though there are several benefits with this method, there are a few things to be away of when working on the regression algorithm. The biggest shortcoming that you will quickly notice is that you aren't able to use this algorithm to help out with any classification problem that comes up. The reason that classification problems and the regression algorithm don't always work together is because this particular algorithm tries to overfit the data many times. So, if you do try to add in different constraints here, you will find that the whole process is going to get tedious pretty quickly.

The clustering algorithms

We spent some time earlier looking at what are known as the clustering algorithms when we talked about the k-means clustering algorithm. But now we are going to dive a bit more into what these clustering algorithms are able to do, and why they are so important to learn all about when you do some machine learning.

When we are able to focus our attention on the clustering algorithms, we have to double check that these are kept simple, rather than adding in a lot of complexity. This method is meant to take on all of the data that you are working with, and then will create some clusters in order to put the points of data together before you start up an algorithm that relies on clustering, you will be able to benefit from choosing the number of clusters that you would like to work with. This is going to depend on how much data you are working with, and what you are planning on finding when the algorithm is done.

Let's say that you are working on a project where you would like to divide up your customers between male and females to start with. This kind of program would just need to have two clusters to sort people out. But if you would like to learn more about the different age groups of your customers, then dividing into five or six clusters could be a bit more useful. After you have been able to implement how many clusters you would like to work with, the program is able to add in the clusters and will make all of the data points fit into there

One of the things you will enjoy about this algorithm is that it is going to be able to take on most of the work that you need to do for you in the process. This is because it is going to take the information that you give about how many clusters you would like to use and then can add in all of the data points to the various clusters based on how they fit. This is going to ensure that the information is easy to read and is organized, and you will be surprised at the insights that you can gain from doing this kind of algorithm.

After the information has been sorted out into the various clusters it is possible that you will take a look at them and notice that there are a lot of different points that show up inside. It is safe to assume that the more points that fall inside a specific cluster, the more likely your target market fits in that group. Remember that the points that fit inside one cluster are going to be similar to one another, while not being similar to the points of data that show up in some of the other clusters that you have.

Once you have formed some of the original clusters, it is time for you to take an individual cluster and divide it up to get more sets of clusters, if this makes sense for what you want to get out of this algorithm. You are able to do this as many times as you want, creating a bunch of divisions as you go through each one. In fact, it is possible to go through these steps so many times that you will stop seeing changes as you do the work.

Now, there are going to be a lot of reasons why a programmer would want to work with these kinds of clustering algorithms when they do some work with machine learning. First, when you use a clustering algorithm to help with your computational work, it is much easier and more cost efficient to get the work done, especially when we look at some of the other options, the supervised learning options, that can do the same thing. And if you plan to work with some problems of classification, then these types of algorithms are the ones to get it all done.

With this in mind, it is important to remember that the clustering algorithm is not going to be the right one to work with every time that you do some machine learning. This algorithm is not going to show you predictions or tell you exactly what to do. You can look at the clusters and figure out some trends and make some decisions, but you have to be the one who does the work at coming up with the course of action.

What is the Markov algorithm?

Another type of unsupervised machine learning algorithm that you can work with is the Markov algorithm. This particular algorithm is going to take the data that you decide to input into it, and then it will translate it to help work in another coding language if you choose.

The nice thing here is that you can pick out which rules you want to use with this algorithm ahead of time so that the algorithm will work the way that you want. Many programmers in machine learning find that this algorithm, and the fact they can set up their own rules ahead of time, is nice because it allows you to take a string of data and ensure that it is as useful as possible as you learn on the job and figure out the parameters of how the data will behave.

Another thing that you may like about this Markov algorithm is that you are able to work with it in several ways, rather than being stuck with just one method. One option to consider here is that this algorithm works well with things like DNA. For example, you could take the DNA sequence of someone, and then use this algorithm to translate the information that is inside that sequence into some numerical values.

This can often make it easier for programmers, doctors, and scientists and more to know what information is present, and to make better predictions into the future. When you are working with programmer and computers, you will find that the numerical data is going to be much easier to sort through than other options of looking through DNA.

A good reason why you would need to use the Markov algorithm is because it is great at learning problems when you already know the input you want to use, but you are not sure about the parameters. This algorithm is going to be able to find insights that are inside of the information. In some cases, these insights are hidden and this makes it hard for the other algorithms we have discussed to find them.

While there are a lot of benefits that can come with working on the Markov algorithm, it is important to know that this one can sometimes prove difficult for some beginners because they do have to go through it manually to create a new rule. This happens when they want to add in a new coding language to the work. If you only plan to work with Python while doing this, you only need to make the rules once and it is not that big of a deal. But if you do plan to work with several coding languages in machine learning at a time, then this could become a big hassle to work with.

Q-learning

We haven't had much of a chance to talk about any of the reinforcement types of machine learning that you are able to work with. This kind of machine learning is going to be a bit different than we would see with some of the other two types, in that it is going to rely mostly on true and false kind of learning rather than on teaching it with examples or letting it learn through the unsupervised machine learning method. This can make it easier for you to train the program how to react in the way that you would like and can ensure that you are going to be able to see how different types of machine learning will work.

With that in mind, it is time to take a look at one of the algorithms that you can do with reinforcement learning known as Q-learning. With this kind of algorithm, you are going to find that it is the most effective, and it is going to work out the best, with something that is described as temporal difference learning.

Compared to a few of the other types of algorithms that we have talked about in this guidebook the Q-learning one would be considered an off-policy algorithm. This is because it is not going to have the abilities inside to learn an action value function. This may sound confusing, but it means that you are going to be able to get the results and the output, regardless of the kind of state you are in at the time.

Since you can take this Q-learning algorithm and use it no matter what function you are trying to create in machine learning, you will first need to take the time and go through your application and list out the specifications that you want to use. These specifications should tell us how the user, or even the learner, is going to select the action they want to take. This can take a bit more time and means you have more steps to do with the process, but it is definitely something that is worth the effort and the time.

After you have been able to go through and actually find all of the functions that are considered action value that you would like to use (read through them and see if they are actually useful for the code that you are writing, it is time for you to create your own optimal policy. One of the best methods that you need in order to construct this is to use the actions that you think would be seen as the highest value for your program, regardless of the kind of state that you would like to work in here.

Just like with any of the other algorithms that we have discussed in this guidebook, there are going to be a few benefits that come with using this algorithm. One of the benefits is that you won't have to worry about taking all of that time, or dealing with all of the effort, to put in the models of the environment in order to get the system to compare it. You can even go with the option of 6choosing to compare a couple different actions, and even many actions, at the same time.

As you can see, there are a lot of different types of algorithms that you are able to use when it comes to artificial intelligence and machine learning, and

Python, as well as a lot of the different libraries and extensions that come with it, are going to be able to help you get this done. Whether you want to work with supervised machine learning, unsupervised machine learning, or reinforcement learning, you are sure to find the results that match up with your chosen project, and what you would like to do.

This guidebook took some time to explore these different parts and to ensure that we know how to make them work. And with all of the options, we can really see how machine learning is going to take off and help us to grow and change technology like never before. Think about all of the cool things that are yet undiscovered, and that we have yet to do, when it comes to working with machine learning with Python.

Conclusion

Thank for making it through to the end of *Python Programming*, let's hope it was informative and able to provide you with all of the tools you need to achieve your goals whatever they may be.

The next step is to take a look at some of the different topics that we discussed in this guidebook. There is a lot of information to process through here and learn about when you want to do some of the various tasks, like machine learning and artificial intelligence, but you also want to be able to work with the ease and the power that comes with the Python coding language.

This guidebook took some time to explore a lot of the different topics that can come up with this. It is meant to help us understand how to work with Python, what is all available with Python, and so much more. And with all of the great libraries and other extensions and features that come with this language, it is no wonder that there are so many things that you are able to do with the help of

Python to make your own machine learning algorithms.

Working with machine learning is something that a lot of different companies want to focus on now. They like the idea of being able to get a system to learn while they are not there. they like to provide a better kind of customer service than they could before. And they like all of the doors and opportunities that are going to present themselves when it comes to this kind of programming. And when they can provide it all and learn how to do all of the different parts with the help of Python, that can just make that much easier.

Finally, if you found this book useful in any way, a review on Amazon is always appreciated!

Copyright © 2019 by Marc Matthes

All rights reserved. No part of this publication may be reproduced, stored in a retrieval system or transmitted, in **any** form or by **any** means, electronic, mechanical, photocopying, recording or otherwise, without permission in writing from the publisher.

www.ingramcontent.com/pod-product-compliance
Lightning Source LLC
Chambersburg PA
CBHW070617220526
45466CB00001B/32